AF841648

QUICKENED

Smith Hughes & Associates Inc.

QUICKENED

Made Alive!

SPIRIT SOUL BODY

Stephanie O. Hughes

Smith Hughes & Associates Inc.
Lansing, Michigan 48915-1759

ISBN 0-9721712-0-7

Library of Congress Control Number 2002093103

First Edition

The information given in this book is not meant to diagnose or override the instructions of your personal physicians. The intent of the writer is to give basic data to develop in the readers an understanding that enhances their knowledge and stimulates a sense of personal responsibility in the pursuit of physical, mental and spiritual health and wellness and strengthen their belief in God's ability to heal and repair the body He created.

DEDICATED TO

Bishop Donald R. Jones
Bishop Emeritus, Original Churches of God
Who taught me to love the pure Word of God from the Old Testament Prophets through Revelations.

Elder Carey A. McLaurine
My father-in-law, who became my pastor and dad.
He taught me the beauty of scripture committed to memory and its power in directing one's life.

Wilbert K. Hughes
My beloved husband who never doubted my ability to complete this project.

IN MEMORY OF

Elder John Henry Smith
My dad, who taught me about compassion, hard work and that I could do anything I set my mind to do.

Evangelist Maude M. Smith
My mother, who showed me faith and God's healing hand on my life.
She taught me to use a Thompson's Chain Reference Bible.

Brother Clarence D. Dowthard
My uncle, a national trustee and teacher in the Original Churches of God.
He showed me how multiple lessons (ancient history and English language) can be taught while teaching the Word of God.
His unpublished Bible lessons enhance this written work.

Brother Elton Howard
My Sunday school teacher and youth group leader during my adolescence.
He required that I research biblical subjects and principles in the Word.

TABLE OF CONTENTS

ILLUSTRATIONS

TABLES

FOREWORD

Stephanie Hughes brings to light the mutual relation of the church, the living Body of Christ, as a spiritual force for rebirth and the health professions, as a bio-social force for a healthy way of life and well-being. Since spirit, soul and body are integral (are three parts of one whole), rebirth and resurrection transform the body as well as the spirit and soul. This means that scientific discoveries in anatomy and physiology share in the divine wisdom revealed by the *risen* Christ and the church as His spiritual body. *QUICKENED* Made Alive! truly takes us on a spiritual odyssey: Many astonishing analogies open our minds to the harmony between scientific knowledge in anatomy and physiology and the Truth revealed to and practiced by the church, as a community firmly established in biblical wisdom.

QUICKENED Made Alive! seeks to enliven our spirit, soul and body as Hughes bridges traditional biblical revelations and modern scientific discoveries in the health professions. With exemplary knowledge of both the heavenly and earthly realms, she seeks to pry open our spiritual depths while deepening our understanding of anatomy and physiology, strengthening our faith, warming our hearts and enlivening our spirit so we "see" the gift, mystery and struggle of life through new "eyes" and with greater appreciation and gratitude. Hughes gives us—students and parents, teachers and preachers—a timeless, precious gift needed in today's world which, able to produce a potential material abundance for all, finds many of us yearning for some-**thing.** In answer to this paradox, ***Quickened*** directs us toward the *Light:* to awaken us to the *Way* so that our lives, rather than conforming to harmful lifestyles, will be graced and fortified—body, soul and spirit.

Vincent L. Lombardi
Professor of Psychology
Michigan State University

PREFACE

This is not meant to be a storybook. It is meant to enlighten and provoke change in the spirit, soul and/or body of the readers. The chapters of this book begin with a single page of anatomy and physiology, which sets the scope for the content of the rest of the chapter. Selected anatomical and physiological functions of the body's systems are utilized to draw parallels between the body, spirit and mind, forming associations in the imaginations of readers. Each chapter builds on information from previous chapters and will be more easily understood if they are read in order. Readers who find the anatomy and physiology page to be cumbersome may skip that page because each physical function of the system is described with spiritual insight in the next section of the chapter. Medical terminology should not be allowed to frustrate the reader. Basic understanding can still be attained if you just keep reading. Chapter summaries were suggested by my son-in-law, Dwayne Holland. They highlight some of the meaningful messages to be gleaned from the chapter.

In a recent preliminary review by the *Literally Speaking Book Club* in Akron, Ohio, *QUICKENED* Made Alive! was found to be relevant and inspirational to a diverse group of readers. These career women were teachers, a beauty shop owner, a nurse, a college administrator, an accountant and my daughter, Rachel, a pastor's administrative assistant. Their denominational affiliations were Catholic, Seventh Day Adventist, Church of God in Christ and Methodist. What a bond of fellowship as we shared one spirit, discussing the Body of Christ and focused on the true ministry of the church. Page 123 was created due to their suggestion.

Read when you have time, and do not try to rush through the material. You will be strengthened. The Scripture references used from the Holy Bible are from The Thompson Chain-Reference King James Bible Fifth Improved Edition and when indicated, the Holy Bible, New International Version (NIV).

ACKNOWLEDGMENTS

Front Cover
Sunrise at the Grand Canyon by Stephanie O. Hughes

Illustrations of Cells
Stephanie O. Hughes

All other illustrations by
Keyna Star Hughes

Editing assistance by
Wordpix Services

Logo and Formatting
Faith Stewart

Thanks for all of the encouraging words, e-mails and excellent advice.
Pastor Geraldine Richardson

Thank you for typing and English lessons, your arguments and encouragement.
You are my gift from God. Some day we'll meet.
Vincent L. Lombardi

Thanks for your influence in the outline stage, a divinely planned meeting in San Francisco.
Marilynn James

Thanks for your prayers.
Pastor Albert Kelley and PAOCOG Members

Thanks for your miscellaneous support.
Sharon Watson

INTRODUCTION

I began utilizing the similarities between our physical bodies and the spiritual Body of Christ as a tool for memorizing basic chemical data while in nursing school. After graduating in 1978, and through many difficult times in my life, these analogies continued to develop in my mind and have been a tremendous source of strength to me. I believe that if I can convey this concept to others, it will help them find and fill their places in the spiritual church. Readers may have an increased capacity of faith for mental and physical healing, they will be able to participate in the growth and effectiveness of the church and enjoy a healthier way of life.

My goals are multiple, enabling a person to: 1) Write so that readers can understand basic anatomy and physiology and principles of health and wellness; 2) stimulate within ministers physical and spiritual analogies that will enhance their sermons; 3) help readers find strength and direction for the spiritual and natural purpose for their lives; 4) lead potential believers to understand the concept of the church as the Body of Christ so that they will find salvation to be an essential ingredient for their lives.

In his letter to the church, John, the beloved disciple, said, "Beloved, I wish above all things that thou mayest prosper and be in health, even as thy soul prospereth." (III John 2). This, too, is my desire for the Body of Christ.

"And God said, Let us make man in our image, after our likeness; ... So God created man in his own image, in the image of God created he him; male and female created he them.... And God saw every thing that he had made, and, behold, it was very good." (Genesis 1:26a, 27a, 31). It is my belief that since God's systematic creation of man brought Him such satisfaction, that he would incorporate certain principles of the physical body into the spiritual Body of Christ, of which He made His son Jesus the head.

Paul, in his letter to the church in Rome, exhorted them to present their bodies as living sacrifices unto God, transformed by renewed minds to prove the good and acceptable and perfect will of God. To accomplish God's perfect will, Paul advised them that they could not think of themselves according to the "class system," in which they would be ranked according to a worldly order of importance. However, if they thought of themselves as members of one physical body, they would have a clearer understanding of the interdependence and synergistic attributes of their positions in the church and would work together more effectively (Romans 12:3,10,16,18). Paul continued this analogy of the church as the Body of Christ in his letters to the Churches located in Corinth, and Ephesus, encouraging them to work together (I Corinthians 12:25) and to be kind and forgiving toward each other (Ephesians 4:32).

This three dimensional book addresses the spirit, soul and body of man. Each of the twelve chapters contains a short description of very basic anatomy and physiology by system; the spiritual implications and similarities; followed by a Pathology and Health and Wellness topic associated with the system.

Tissues are groups of similar cells that are joined together to perform specific functions. Organs are made of similar tissues that perform a particular function. (Examples of organs are the heart, liver, lungs, brain and stomach). An association of organs that have a common function is called a body system. There are ten systems in the body that work together to make a normal functioning body. From these human body systems comparisons are drawn between the physical body and the spiritual Body of Christ.

Believers having similar beliefs form a church. Within the church membership are organizations of believers who perform specific functions (missionaries, ushers, choir etc). Churches that have similar interests form associations and denominations. All Bible-believing churches together form the spiritual Body of Christ. Jesus told his disciples, "And other sheep I have, which are not of this fold: them also I must bring, and they shall hear my voice; and there shall be one fold, and one shepherd." (John 10:16)

Allow me to clarify my visualization and interpretation of the Body of Christ. It is not that beaten, forsaken, limp, dead physical body that Joseph of Arimathaea took from the cross and carried to the tomb for burial. From this point forward, when I reference the Body of Christ, I will be referring to the body of the *risen* Christ. This body is alive and well. It is spiritual, appears anywhere, is all-powerful and invincible. This is the Body of Christ that Luke, the beloved physician, wrote about while observing the apostle Paul minister to the church. "For in him we live, and move, and have our being; ... For we are also his offspring." (Acts 17:28)

Much too often, churches just *survive*. That is, members make it through Sunday and weeknight services, the choirs sing and pastors preach the congregations to an emotional high. Some members even visit the sick. People "survive" storms but suffer great losses. An unconscious person with a severe closed head injury "survived" the trauma but is non-functional. The Body of Christ in this book is a *thriving* 24 hour 7 day per week spiritual body in which every individual is vital and knows his/her function. They exude the characteristics of the Spirit of Christ, know the Word and are physically and mentally whole.

"And the Lord God formed man of the dust of the ground, and breathed into his nostrils the breath of life; and man became a living soul." (Genesis 2:7) When God created Adam, He breathed the breath of life into his nostrils. As soon as God's breath came into contact with man's body, the human spirit was produced. God's breath became man's spirit, the earth's elements became man's body and the union of these two produced the soul. The soul, also called the mind, heart, intellect, intelligence of man, became the linking agent between the spirit world and the flesh. It receives, evaluates, discards or accepts messages between the spirit and body, making the decisions that affect the whole man.[1] The *quickened spirit* is enthusiastic, excitable, active and motivated, responding and connecting to God. The *quickened soul* is focused and content, making appropriate decisions for the well-being of the spirit and body. The *quickened body* is one that is disciplined by the soul and spirit and functions in a state of health and wellness. The apostle Paul told the church, "I pray God your whole spirit and soul and body be preserved blameless unto the coming of our Lord Jesus Christ." (I Thessalonians 5:23b)

The spiritual Body of Christ, the church, is disciplined by the spirit of God and functions in a state of health and wellness when the minds of believers are focused on God's purpose for the church. This spiritual Body of Christ must flourish on this earth. It must grow, flex its muscles by the power of God and respond to the environment. It must influence the outcomes of the evil that surrounds us in the world by example, through prayer, one on one and at the voting polls. Throughout these chapters, readers will identify with the spiritual, physical and emotional truths, finding and enhancing a *quickened* way of life.

---

[1] International Bible Institute and Seminary Tyler Crusades Inc. 1966 Series 3 GT45; pages 2&3.

CHAPTER ONE
The Cell

The cell is the basic unit of structure for all plants and animals. It is a mass of protoplasm with organic elements that contain a nucleus or nuclear material, surrounded by a cell wall. The cell operates independently and in harmony with other cells. From this point forward, the use of the word cells will refer to human body cells and not those of plants or animals. Cells and the products of cells comprise all tissues of the body.

Characteristics of Cells:

- The nucleus of a cell directs its functions. It contains DNA, the genetic makeup of human organisms. DNA establishes the identity and unique characteristics or peculiarities that make us distinct individuals.

- Cells produce other cells much like themselves, as one cell divides into two. The nucleus of the cell reproduces identical portions of DNA, then it divides with the cell wall, making two cells. This process is repeated over and over, resulting in growth of the organism.

- Cells arise only from pre-existing cells.

- The structure and form of a cell are closely correlated with its function: Bone cells, blood cells, tissue, muscle, glandular, nervous and brain cells etc. The configuration of each type of cell is different, depending on the purpose it will serve in the body. Bone cells are designed to form strong structures; muscular cells can stretch and contract; and nerve cells have tentacles that extend to touch other cells.

- All functional activities of the body are carried on by cells: For instance, to make a person eat, run, frown, smile etc., each cell must function independently and work cooperatively with other cells to accomplish the mission at hand.

- Growth and development of the body are the result of an increase in numbers of cells and the differentiation of cells into various types of tissues.

- Cells grow in cycles, going through specific developmental periods or phases, resulting in a mature cell, ready for cell division. At any given time, our bodies contain cells at various stages of development.

- Cells have the power to exercise the vital processes of life. They are equipped with the ability to allow nourishment to enter and waste to exit through the cell wall; and they have the ability to convert raw materials from the external environment into energy. Cells can store nutrients and transport them to other cells, and some even move around.[1]

CELLS

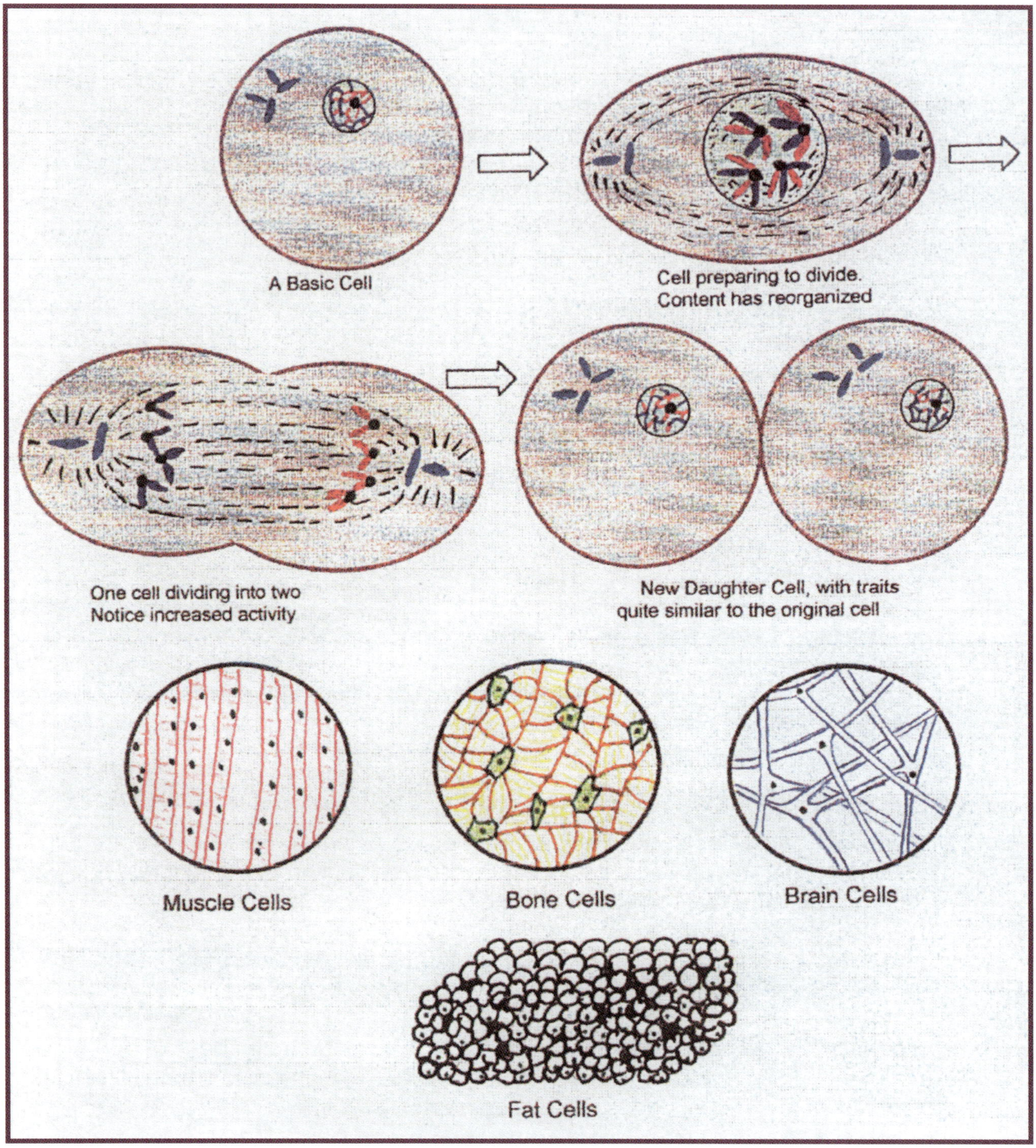

[1] Gerard J. Tortora and Nicholas Anagnostakos, Principles of Anatomy and Physiology (San Francisco: Canfield Press, 1975), pp. 38-56

THE CELL: **A Born Again Individual**

Prior to spiritual birth, individuals exist in this world oblivious to the fact that to have completeness and fulfillment in their lives, they must come to terms with their spiritual purpose on this earth. Paul described this oblivious state of being to the church of Ephesus: "At that time ye were without Christ, being aliens from the commonwealth of Israel, and strangers from the covenants of promise, having no hope, and without God in the world." (Ephesians 2:12)

After experiencing the spiritual birth, an individual:

1. Has the Spirit of Christ.
2. Is a citizen of the commonwealth of Israel.
3. Is heir to the covenants of promise.
4. Has hope.
5. Has God.

WE HAVE THE SPIRIT OF CHRIST

"Hereby we know that he abideth in us, by the Spirit which he hath given us." (I John 3:24b) The new believer has the indwelling identity of Christ, like DNA, imprinted on his/her life. The Spirit of Christ is the common denominator in the Body of Christ that unites believers to one another and to Christ, making them members of one body. Believers are the basic unit of structure in the Body of Christ just as a cell is the basic unit of structure in the human body.

As DNA establishes our identity and unique characteristics, The Spirit of Christ within us identifies our characteristics as members of the Body of Christ. Characteristics of the Spirit of Christ include: wisdom and understanding, counsel and might, knowledge and fear of the Lord; being righteous, just, fearless and faithful (Isaiah 11:2-5). The Spirit of Christ is also tender (Isaiah 40:11), quiet, gentle and persevering (Isaiah 42:2-4), liberating (Isaiah 61:1), saving (Isaiah 63:1), compassionate (Matthew 9:36), meek and lowly (Matthew 11:29), longsuffering (Luke 9:55-56), forgiving (Luke 23:34), zealous (Acts 10:38), burden-bearing (Galatians 6:2) and loving (Ephesians 5:2).

WE ARE CITIZENS OF THE COMMONWEALTH OF ISRAEL

"But now thus saith the Lord that created thee, O Jacob, and he that formed thee, O Israel, fear not: for I have redeemed thee, I have called thee by thy name; thou art mine. When thou passest through the waters, I will be with thee; and through the rivers, they shall not overflow thee: when thou walkest through the fire, thou shalt not be burned; neither shall the flame kindle upon thee. For I am the Lord thy God, the Holy One of Israel, thy Savior." (Isaiah 43:1-3a) This was God's covenant with the nation of Israel while they were under the dispensation of the law in the Old Testament. In the New Testament, the spiritual birth makes sons and daughters of all who believe, and they become God's chosen people and heirs to the commitments God made to Israel. "But when the time had fully come, God sent his son, born of a woman, born under law, to redeem those under law, that we might receive the full rights of sons. Because you are sons, God sent the Spirit of his Son into our hearts, the spirit who calls out "Abba, Father." .. And since you are a son, God has made you also an heir." (Galatians 4:4-6,7bNIV)

WE INHERIT THE COVENANT OF PROMISE

That describes the permanently blessed life that is available to those who have the Spirit of Christ. In His covenant with Abraham, God said, "I will make you into a great nation and I will bless you; I will make your name great, and you will be a blessing. I will bless those who bless you, and whoever curses you I will curse; and all peoples on earth will be blessed through you." (Genesis 12:2-3NIV).

WE HAVE HOPE

The psalmist said, "Happy is he that hath the God of Jacob for his help, whose hope is in the Lord his God." (Psalm 146:5) Hope is knowing that current life situations do not have to remain as they are. With God, there is the expectation that things will change for the better, and that on a day known only to Him, we will go to live with him. "For the Lord himself shall descend from heaven with a shout, with the voice of the archangel, and with the trump of God: and the dead in Christ shall rise first: Then we which are alive and remain shall be caught up together with them in the clouds, to meet the Lord in the air: and so shall we ever be with the Lord." (I Thessalonians 4:16,17)

WE HAVE GOD

The psalmist also said, "God is our refuge and strength, a very present help in trouble." (Psalm 46:1) Jesus told Nicodemus, "That which is born of the flesh is flesh; and that which is born of the Spirit is spirit. Marvel not that I say unto thee, Ye must be born again." (John 3:6-7) Physical birth makes us part of our physical families (flesh); Spiritual birth makes us part of God's spiritual family and members of the Body of Christ, His son.

Believers have a responsibility in the Body of Christ, to grow to spiritual maturity, to take part in the functional activities of the church, to stimulate the birth of more believers and to be available to be used by Christ to contribute to the growth of the church. Since these responsibilities are quite similar to the list of characteristics of the human cell, we will examine them more closely in light of the believer's responsibilities in the Body of Christ and as members of the family of God.

Human cells produce cells much like themselves. The attributes of the Spirit of Christ show through the lives of born again individuals to the darkness in this world like a candle that is set on a hill. These attributes are a pattern for others to admire and desire to duplicate in their own lives. Through these characteristics and the loving kindness of God, non-believers are drawn to Him through believers. Thus, one cell makes a second, third and so on. "Let your light so shine before men, that they may see your good works, and glorify your Father which is in heaven." (Matthew 5:16)

REALITY CHECK: If your church included several members like yourself, how effective would it be in the community?

Cells arise only from pre-existing cells. Non-believers are converted through the example set by the way of life of believers. Paul said, "I magnify mine office: If by any means I may provoke to emulation them which are my flesh, and might save some of them." (Romans 11:13b, 14) By taking his ministry seriously and being a living example to others, he hoped to stimulate in them a desire to be saved like himself.

The structure and form of a cell is closely correlated with its function. Although believers are born of the same spirit, they have different interests and talents that cause them to gravitate to various positions in the Body of Christ. In the New Testament Church, the members were competitive and jealous of one another because of their differences. That is why Christ, through Paul, gave them the analogy of the church being the Body of Christ, in which every person was important and everyone's contribution to the church was vital.

There are many tasks to be done in the church, and members must take an interest and participate in some capacity as a viable entity of the Body of Christ. Cells in our natural bodies that are not viable—living and developing—die. If not appropriately discarded, dead cells cause an infection. Look around the building and at the people. Find a need and fill it. "Whatsoever thy hand findeth to do, do it with thy might." (Ecclesiastes 9:10a).

All functional activities of the body are carried on by cells. Believers must visualize the Body of Christ as a living organism in the community. It is our duty to fulfill our specific purpose within the church and work in cooperation with others to carry out the purpose of the church in this world. What is the purpose of the church, you ask? The church must carry out the mission Jesus came to fulfill on the earth. On his visit to the synagogue in Nazareth, Jesus read from the book of Isaiah, "The spirit of the Lord God is upon me, because he hath anointed me to preach the gospel to the poor; he hath sent me to heal the brokenhearted, to preach deliverance to the captives, and recovering of sight to the blind, to set at liberty them that are bruised, To preach the acceptable year of the Lord." (Luke 4:18-19) & (Isaiah 61:1-3).

Cells have the power to exercise the vital processes of life. The vital processes of life involve taking in nourishment, breaking it down for use by the body, producing energy, storing nutrients, sharing nutrients, procreating and the ability to move and respond to the environment. Believers have the power and responsibility to carry out the vital processes of the Body of Christ: To grow spiritually, reproduce and respond to the environment.

Growth and development of the body is the result of the increase in numbers of cells and the differentiation of cells into various types of tissues. Growth of the church is a result of members bringing people into the church, leading them to Christ and retaining them within the congregation and/or the spiritual Body of Christ. People remain with specific congregations because a need or desire is met. They need to have opportunities to observe all of the ministries in the church, make selections and receive training to participate in the ministries in which they are interested.

Responsibilities in the church progressively outlined list opportunities for new members that give them the chance to participate in the operation of the church while getting acclimated to their new way of life as believers. Lawn work, snow removal, helping out in the kitchen or nursery and assisting in the upkeep of the building are some entry-level tasks. While doing these tasks, newer members have a chance to get to know people in the church and observe other ministries. The next step for the developing believer may be to train for the usher board or to be a missionary, while spiritually growing, then progress to the choir or devotional leader if interested and so on. Our new members should not sit and remain stagnant while the church continues to be busy around them. Biblical and organizational training is necessary in the church so that believers can learn their position in the congregation and then work their position in Christ, beyond the church—in the world.

Cells grow in cycles, going through specific periods or phases. Believers grow spiritually in stages. From the status of newly acquired salvation, we develop a thirst for knowledge and become confident that we are in the family of God because of our faith and belief. Then we learn to satisfy our spiritual hunger and thirst via the Word of God. As we notice changes in our attitude and purpose in life, we are secure with the Spirit of Christ dwelling within us. As knowledge of the Word grows in us daily, we feel safe because we know we are citizens of the commonwealth of Israel. Learning about the covenants of promise, we feel included, accepted, loved and a sense of belonging. We have hope and know that God is working on our behalf in this world. Where there was no confidence, we develop confidence and self-esteem, knowing we can achieve, be competent and gain spiritual approval and recognition in the Body of Christ. These stages of growth take various amounts of time for each individual, from weeks to literally years.

The next step for Christians is to enjoy a fully victorious lifestyle. This cannot happen until all of the previous stages have been accomplished. In a victorious life, one finds spiritual fulfillment and realizes his/her potential. Finally, Christians—believers—reach the level when they can lead others to find that same spiritual fulfillment and experience victories in their lives. The writer encouraged the believers in the Hebrew church to grow to maturity and not to keep circling around and around in discussions about doctrine of Christ, repentance from dead work and faith toward God. (Hebrews 6:1).

THE CELL: **Self – Actualization to Transcendence**

Readers who are still with me at this point realize that merely due to the fact that cells exist in our human bodies, they have duties to perform to keep the physical body healthy. Likewise, believers have responsibilities to fulfill to keep the spiritual Body of Christ healthy and active. Furthermore, even though we are people on this earth by no action or intentions of our own, we are obligated to achieve our highest level of personal growth and satisfaction. We must fulfill our place in the lives of those close to us and in society. To reach this level in life requires that we find self-esteem, self-acceptance and self-responsibility.

Abraham Maslow,[2] known for his contributions to the field of psychology during the 1950's, proposed a hierarchy of human needs, based on two groupings: 1)personal deficiency needs and 2.)growth needs. Although there is little agreement in the world of psychology about the identification of basic human needs and how they are ordered, we can utilize Maslow's basic view of a human being's nature to gain valuable insight to how to work with others and have expectations of ourselves.

According to Maslow, people's *personal needs* can be categorized as:

1. Physical: Hunger, thirst, bodily comforts etc.
2. Safety/Security: We want to live comfortably, feeling safe from danger
3. Belongingness and Love: We want to affiliate with others, be accepted
4. Esteem: We want to achieve, be competent, gain approval and recognition

[2] Huitt, William G., http://chiron.valdosta.edu/whuitt/col/regsys/maslow.html last modified March, 2002

His theory was that within this list of needs, individuals must meet each lower need—starting at number one, before moving to the next higher level.

Once the personal needs are met, the following *psychological growth* can take place:

5. Cognitive: To know, to understand and explore
6. Aesthetic: To appreciate symmetry, order and beauty

We cannot teach others, expecting them to follow our example, memorize factual data, or appreciate a pretty flower or the symmetry of an architectural structure, while they have physical feelings of hunger, fear, ostracism or poor self-esteem, noted in steps 1-4.

Once psychological growth has been established, the next step in Maslow's hierarchy is:

7. Self Actualization, characterized by:
    - Being problem-focused;
    - Having an ongoing freshness and appreciation of life;
    - A concern about personal growth; and
    - The ability to have peak experiences and accomplishments.

Problem solving, motivation to approach each day as an opportunity, setting goals for personal growth and planning experiences beyond the normal day to day occurrences are more difficult for persons who do not appreciate order or have the motivation to explore the unknown in steps 5 and 6.

By utilizing these basic steps in Maslow's Hierarchy of needs, we can assess our own level of growth and specify our mental, physical and spiritual needs. We must determine our current level of growth—for some, identify the point where our growth became stagnant and how unhealthy behaviors can be reversed—then proceed to the next step.

The stair step illustration of Maslow's "hierachy of needs" (Table 1) is a visualization of the personal and psychological growth that takes place in individuals as their needs are realized. Spiritual growth takes place in steps or stages also, and the current stage of growth or level of need an individual is experiencing determines the style of approach others must use to reach them. A stranger who arrives in your home, church or work environment thirsty and needing to visit the restroom is not going to feel accepted or like being a team member until shown the facilities and offered refreshments—for their personal needs. People whom we bring into our congregations from other cultural or financial environments must be made to feel approval and acceptance before we can teach them to understand or memorize the scriptures. A hungry spouse coming home from a tiring day at work will not listen as attentively to your voice before dinner as he/she would after dinner.

Under Maslow's ultimate level of growth and beyond self actualization is:

8. Transcendence:
    - To help others find self-fulfillment and realize their potential.
    - The psychologist G. Marian Kinget, building on Maslow's work, identifies transcendence as a major attribute of being human. Transcendence, she notes, is manifested as an urge to move from ordinary dimensions of thought and action to an awareness of extraordinary dimensions of existence and radically novel perspectives on the cosmos.[3] For Kinget (as for Maslow) the

---

[3] G. Marian Kinget, On Being Human: A Systematic View (New York: Harcourt Brace Jovanovich, Inc., 1975), pg. 218

capacity for transcendence has to do with the spiritual capacity of humans to enter into the realm of meaning—the Kingdom of God.

Jesus said, "I must preach the kingdom of God to other cities also: for therefore am I sent." (Luke 4:43) We know that we have reached the level of spiritual transcendence—maturity in Christ—when we have confidence in our spirituality and can lead others to Christ.

8. Transcendence – Help others realize their potential
7. Self-Actualization – Being problem focused; ongoing freshness and appreciation of life; ability to have peak experiences and life accomplishments
6. Aesthetic Needs – To appreciate symmetry, order and beauty
5. Cognitive Needs - The need to explore and understand
4. Esteem Needs – To achieve and gain approval
3. Belongingness & Love Needs – Accepted by others
2. Safety Needs – Out of danger
1. Physical Needs – Hunger, thirst, bodily comforts

Table 1 Stages of growth: 1-4 Personal Needs; 5-7 Psychological; 8 Beyond Self

Transcendence is attained when we are helping others realize their potential. It could mean teaching a disabled person to read or to swim; helping an addicted person overcome problems of substance abuse; a stuttering person to speak fluently; or leading a person from spiritual birth to a stage of spiritual maturity.

For believers to activate the Body of Christ in the community, members must assess the needs of the community, select one in which they feel an ability to intervene, explore solutions and then apply the most appropriate one in the most effective manner. As Jesus sent workers out into the world, he said "The harvest truly is great, but the labourers are few: pray ye therefore the Lord of the harvest, that he would send forth labourers into his harvest." (Luke 10:2) An exercise on this level brings about spiritual and personal fulfillment. We cannot bring children or adults into our lives or the church and expect them to grow emotionally or spiritually without attending to their basic needs for food, security etc. Fulfilling the need *is* the ministry of the church.

CHAPTER SUMMARY

CELLS AND BELIEVERS:

- Cells have DNA, and believers have the Spirit of Christ that makes them unique.
- Cells and believers reproduce others much like themselves.
- Cells multiply from pre-existing cells as believers multiply because of other believers.
- Cells and believers are configured differently based on the purpose they will serve in the body.
- All functional activities of the body are carried on by cells and believers.
- Growth and development of the body are the result of the increase and maturing of cells and believers in the body.
- Cells and believers mature in developmental stages.
- Cells and believers have the power to exercise the vital processes of life and of the church, the Body of Christ.

SELF – ACTUALIZATION TO TRANSCENDENCE

Abraham Maslow's theory gives an order of personal needs that must be satisfied before more advanced stages of growth can take place in people. They are:

- Personal: Safety / security , belonging and love, esteem.
- Psychological: Cognitive and aesthetic.

We should strive to attain the ultimate stages, which are:

- Self -Actualization – Problem focused and a concern for personal growth.
- Transcendence – Able to help others find self-fulfillment and realize their potential.
- On a personal and organizational level, this means we must recognize the needs and stages of growth in ourselves and in others, to be able to effectively intervene.

CHAPTER TWO
Blood and Lymph Fluid

Blood inside blood vessels, interstitial fluid around body cells and lymph inside lymph vessels constitute the internal environment of the human organism. Blood is the red, thick, sticky fluid that flows through the veins and arteries of the body. It constitutes about eight percent of the total body weight, amounting to approximately five to six quarts in an average-sized male. Interstitial fluid bathes body cells. Lymph, found in lymphatic vessels, picks up wastes from the interstitial fluid, cleanses it of bacteria, and returns the wastes to the blood for disposal.

Some of the important functions of blood are:

1. The transportation of oxygen from the lungs to all cells of the body.
2. The transportation of nutrients from the digestive organs to the cells of the body.
3. The transportation of hormones from endocrine glands to cells of the body.
4. The transportation of enzymes to various cells of the body.
5. The transportation of carbon dioxide from the cells to the lungs.
6. The transportation of waste products from cells to the lymph vascular system and then to the kidneys.
7. The regulation of body pH–the measure of acidity or alkalinity of the blood, seven being neutral increasing to fourteen with increasing alkalinity and decreasing to zero with increasing acidity.
8. The regulation of normal body temperature because it contains such a large volume of water (an excellent heat absorber and coolant).
9. The regulation of the water content of cells.
10. The prevention of body fluid loss through the clotting mechanism.
11. Protection against toxins and foreign microbes through special combat-unit cells in the blood and lymph.

All cells and tissues of the body are kept alive and maintained by blood. It keeps the internal environment of the body relatively constant, a concept referred to as homeostasis, meaning balanced. Homeostasis is necessary for maintenance of life. Among the substances in extracellular fluid are gases, nutrients and electrically charged chemical articles called ions. This fluid moves into the spaces between the tissues and inside blood vessels as plasma. It is called the internal environment of the body.[1]

RED BLOOD CELLS

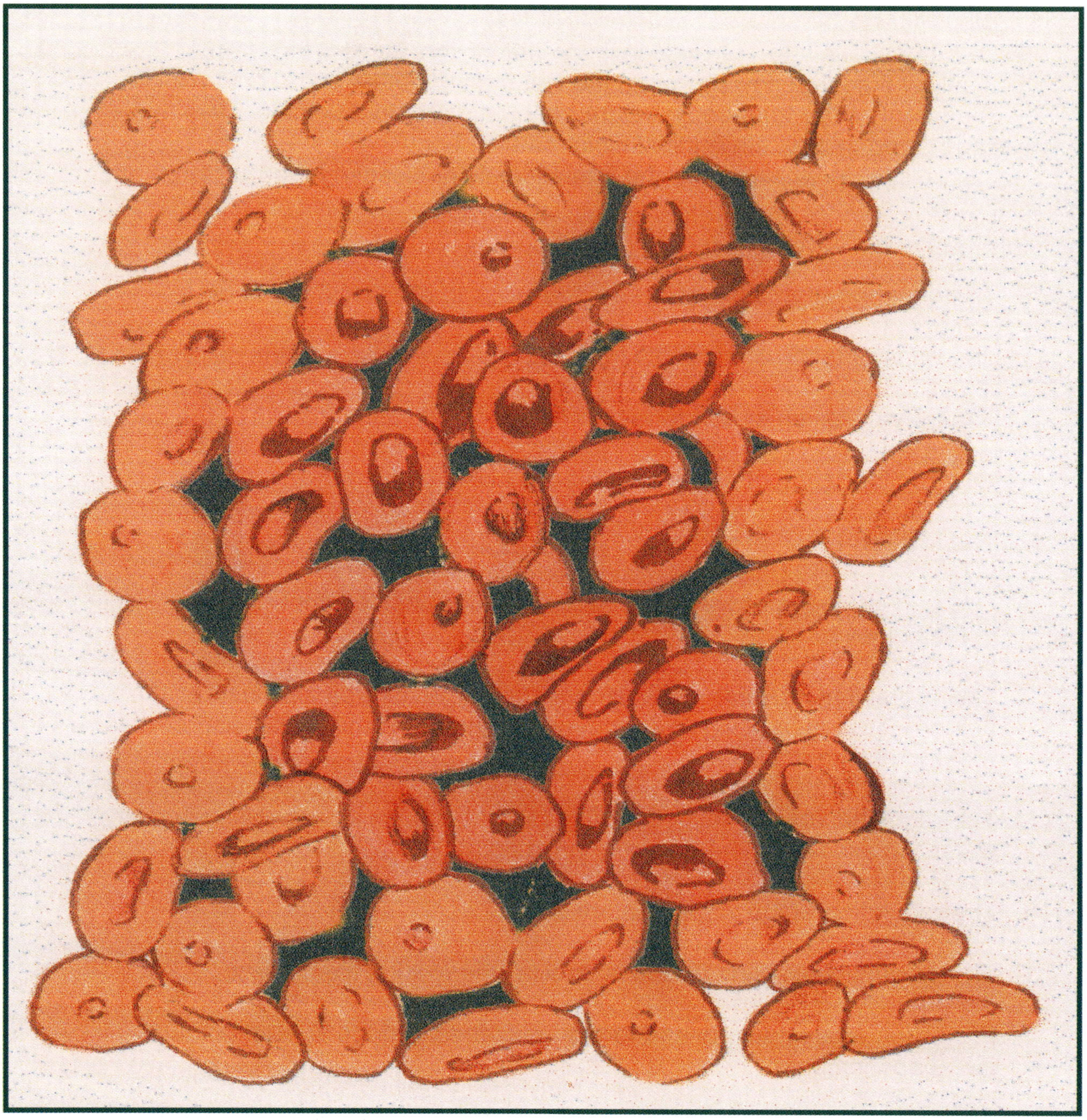

[1] Gerard J. Tortora and Nicholas Anagnostakos, Principles of Anatomy and Physiology (San Francisco: Canfield Press, 1975), pp. 345-352

BLOOD AND LYMPH FLUID: **The Word Of God, Our Spiritual Food**

The scriptures contain several mysteries, one of which is found in the book of John. "In the beginning was the Word, and the Word was with God, and the Word was God. The same was in the beginning with God..... And the Word was made flesh, and dwelt among us." (John 1:1- 2, 14a) God is a complex being with several entities. He is the Father, the Son and the Holy Spirit. In this section, we will focus on the Son, whom we know as Jesus. In the scriptures, Jesus is the Word. Jesus told his disciples, "I am the way, the truth, and the life: no man comes to the father, but by me. If you had known me, you should have known my Father also: ... If you have seen me you have seen the father also: and from now on, consider yourselves to have seen the Father." (John 14:6,7,9b paraphrased). The Word of God consists of Jesus, truth, light, power and life. Blood is red blood cells, white blood cells and plasma. Both the blood and the Word provide life and maintain the internal environment of the natural body and the spiritual Body of Christ.

Adam and Eve enjoyed their lives in spiritual unity with God in the Garden of Eden. One day they disobeyed Him, so God removed them from the garden and removed his spirit from them, and they experienced spiritual death. The Bible tells us that as a result of their disobedience, "death passed upon all men" (Romans 5:12) so since then, all of humanity has been born without the spirit of God. To correct this void, God made and carried out a *plan of salvation*, in which He had the "Word" that was with him in heaven, become flesh in the form of the baby Jesus. As Jesus grew, lived and taught on this earth, he became our perfect example of the profound impact God could make upon the world when there was a spiritual relationship between individuals, God, the Word and the Holy Spirit.

As blood contains the nutrients, oxygen and cleansing agents needed for the cells of the body to maintain its homeostasis—balance, so the Word of God supplies the needs of believers in the spiritual Body of Christ. In Paul's letter to Timothy, he said, "All scripture is given by inspiration of God, and is profitable for doctrine, for reproof, for correction, for instruction in righteousness: That the man of God may be perfect, thoroughly furnished unto all good works." (II Timothy 3:16) The Holy Scriptures provide the tools that believers need to grow to spiritual maturity and assign structure in the church to maintain order and homeostasis—balance—in the Body of Christ.

The functions of the blood described on page eleven, are those necessary to perpetuate human life. In the scriptures Jesus said, "I am come that they might have life, and that they might have it more abundantly." (John 10:10b) "In him was life; and the life was the light of men." (John 1:4) Here, John referred to Jesus, the Son of God. A true meaningful life for us comes from knowing *Him* through the scriptures, and this knowledge sheds light (understanding) on our lives.

By knowing Jesus and the principles of the gospel, we become aware of Gods' many great and precious promises, pertaining to life and godliness. All of these promises give us grace and peace multiplied, and God's divine nature (II Peter 1: 2-4 paraphrased). So, the Word is to the spirit and soul of believers as blood is to the cells of our bodies.

BLOOD TRANSPORTS SUBSTANCES *TO* THE CELLS:

1. Blood takes oxygen from the lungs to the cells to refresh or renew them. Similarly, reading and obeying the Word **renews** the spirit and soul of believers. Paul, in his letter to the church at Corinth, said, "Though our outward man perish, yet the inward man is renewed day by day." (II Corinthians 4:16b)

2-3. Blood transports nutrients from the digestive system to the cells for repair and delivers hormones to the cells for growth. The Word of God gives us nutrients to **repair** our broken spirits. The Psalmist, who had been afraid and depressed, recovered and gave his testimony that "He healeth the broken in heart, and bindeth up their wounds." (Psalm 147:3)

The Word stimulates in us a desire to change, allowing spiritual and emotional **growth**. Peter told the church, "As newborn babes, desire the sincere milk of the Word, that ye may grow thereby." (I Peter 2:2) "Grow in grace, and in the knowledge of our Lord and Savior Jesus Christ." (II Peter 3:18)

4. Enzymes are transported to cells to break down substances in the cells for waste. **Truth** is the spiritual enzyme of the Word that, when taught with **love**, breaks down our hardened hearts to change, grow and love one another. "But speaking the truth in love, may grow up into him in all things, which is the head, even Christ." (Ephesians 4:15) "And so we know and rely on the love God has for us. God is love. Whoever lives in love lives in God, and God in him." (I John 4:16 NIV) "We know that we have passed from death unto life, because we love the brethren. "(I John 3:14)

BLOOD TRANSPORTS SUBSTANCES *FROM* THE CELLS:

5-6. Cells release carbon dioxide into the blood where it is transported to the lungs for disposal. Other waste by-products are released into the lymph system and carried to the kidneys for disposal. God, in his infinite wisdom, provided methods for the body to rid itself of the waste, or by-products of this perfectly functioning machine.

Similarly, the Word of God will **clean** our thoughts, attitudes and habits if we allow it to eliminate those that are harmful to our emotional and/or spiritual growth. King David said, "Wherewithal shall a young man cleanse his way? By taking heed thereto according to thy word." (Psalm 119:9). "Create in me a clean heart, O God; and renew a right spirit within me." (Psalm 51:10) Jesus told his disciples, "Now ye are clean through the word which I have spoken unto you." (John 15:3).

BLOOD REGULATES THE BODY'S INTERNAL ENVIRONMENT:

7-9. Blood regulates our body pH by the level of acid it contains. It also regulates body temperature and the amount of fluid the cells absorb. The Word **regulates** our entire being, maintaining homeostasis, which is harmony, in our spirit, soul and body. "And every man that striveth for the mastery is temperate in all things." (I Corinthians 9:25) "For the word of God is living and active. Sharper than any double-edged sword, it penetrates even to dividing soul and spirit, joints and marrow; it judges the thoughts and attitudes of the heart." (Hebrews 4:12NIV)

BLOOD HAS PROPERTIES OF PREVENTION:

*10. The blood's clotting mechanism **prevents** excessive blood loss*. Sometimes when the Word of God is being spoken, it seems that nothing is being understood or no one is listening, similar to profuse bleeding. But not to worry God's word has a purpose, and that purpose will be served. God told Isaiah, "So shall my word be that goeth forth out of my mouth: it shall not return unto me void, but it shall accomplish that which I please, and it shall prosper in the thing whereto I sent it." (Isaiah 55:11) When a scripture or illustration spoken by a believer stays in the thoughts of another, a type of "clot" forms, and the word builds on the thought, taking root, gradually eliminating the desire for evil and accomplishes the purpose for which it was sent.

BLOOD PROTECTS THE BODY:

*11. Finally, the body is **protected** against toxins and foreign microbes through special combat cells in the blood and lymph*. "And take the helmet of salvation, and the sword of the spirit, which is the word of God." (Ephesians 6:17) "As the mountains are round about Jerusalem, so the Lord is round about his people from henceforth even for ever." (Psalm 125:2) God arms believers with power and protects them in the time of trouble.

In Jesus' prayer prior to his crucifixion he said, "My prayer is not that you take them *out* of the world but that you *protect* them from the evil one. They are not of the world, even as I am not of it. Sanctify them by the truth; your word is truth." (John 17:15-17NIV) To "sanctify" means to set apart for a special purpose. When I was a child, my mother had "special" dishes that were to be used only when we had company. These dishes were "sanctified." They had a special purpose.

BLOOD AND LYMPH FLUID ■ PATHOLOGY
Bloodborne Diseases

Bloodborne Diseases – HIV AIDS

Human blood in its purest state provides all that the body needs to maintain life. However, due to indiscretions of individuals, the wholesomeness of blood can be compromised by disease organisms. Since these disease organisms *live only in human blood and bodily fluids*, they are called bloodborne diseases. They pass from person to person when blood or bodily fluids from an infected person gets into the mouth, mucous membranes or openings in the skin of another person. There is no risk of disease to anyone who has casual contact with a person having a bloodborne disease.

The Human Immunodeficiency Virus (HIV) is a bloodborne disease organism that has gained a lot of notoriety over the past decades. The HIV virus gets into the blood and cripples the natural cells that fight off disease. Not only does the HIV virus keep these cells from fighting disease; it causes them to destroy each other. A person's diagnosis changes from "Positive HIV" to "AIDS" once the number of cells that fight disease—CD4 lymphocytes—are reduced to a certain level[2]. The body is then defenseless against diseases like pneumonia, skin and brain cancers and tuberculosis. Yes, there are medications that are prescribed to lengthen life, but the person's quality of life is often compromised due to side effects of the medications. There is no cure for the disease yet. Death is not due to AIDS but to the diseases one acquires because of the body's lack of resistance to them.

The intriguing thing about the diagnosis of positive HIV is that one can have it for years without symptoms or without a test confirming the disease. Meanwhile, they pass the disease on to others. Some, although fully aware of their disease state, continue to practice "at risk" behaviors, exposing others to the disease believing that "it is only fair" because they themselves were unknowingly exposed to the disease at one time.

REALITY CHECK: A destructive process similar to that of AIDS can occur in group relationships and business projects also. Imagine a group of people working together in the occupational or religious environment. Add a diverse individual or a controversial subject to the group. Failure to utilize the universal precaution of love and respect for each other will result in disputes that destroy relationships in the group. Then the mission and goals of the group are laid aside while people quash each other spiritually, psychologically and sometimes physically. The purpose for the group is destroyed, the mission and goals of the group die, and nothing is accomplished while members go their separate ways nursing their pain. Paul described this process to the church, "The entire law is summed up in a single command: 'Love your neighbor as yourself.' If you keep on biting and devouring each another, watch out or you will be destroyed by each other." (Galatians 5:14,15NIV)

Bloodborne Diseases - Hepatitis B

Hepatitis B is an inflammatory disease caused by the hepatitis B virus (HBV) that results in damaged liver cells. It can lead to scarring of the liver (cirrhosis) and increases the risk of liver cancer in some people. Over 200,000 people get hepatitis B each year.

Transmission: Hepatitis B virus is found in blood, seminal fluid and vaginal secretions. Like HIV, it can be spread by:

- Sexual contact with an infected person.
- Contact with infected body fluids and contaminated needles, including tattoo and body piercing instruments.
- Infected mother to newborn at time of delivery.
- Those living in the same household with an infected individual are at risk of being infected.
- Hepatitis is 100 times more contagious and easier to get then HIV.[3]

---

[2] Lawrence M. Tierney Jr., Stephen J. McPhee, Maxine A. Papadakis & Associate Authors Current Medical Diagnosis and Treatment 2002 Forty First Edition (Toronto: Lange/McGraw-Hill Medical Publishing Division, 2002), pp. 1323-1325

[3] Ibid., pp. 678-685

Symptoms:

- Many people with newly acquired hepatitis B have no symptoms at all, or symptoms may be very mild and flu-like: loss of appetite, nausea, fatigue, muscle or joint aches, mild fever, and some may become jaundiced (yellow colored skin).
- The only way to know if you are currently infected or carry the virus is to be tested by your doctor.

Two things can happen to people infected with the Hepatitis B Virus:

1. Develop Immunity :
   - 95% of adults infected develop antibodies and recover spontaneously within six months. Upon recovery they develop immunity to the virus, and they are not infectious to others.[2]
   - Blood tests will test positive for HBV antibody.
   - Blood banks will not accept donations of blood from these individuals.

2. Become chronically infected: If the virus has not been cleared from the body within six months, a person is considered a carrier or chronically infected.
   - The chronically infected may show no signs or symptoms.
   - The virus remains in blood and body fluids and can infect others.
   - Blood banks will not accept donations of blood from these individuals.

Vaccines:

- All newborns and children up to the age of 19 should be vaccinated for hepatitis B. Others who are at risk and should be vaccinated are those who: 1.) Are in positions where they are exposed to blood at work, 2.) Are drug users, 3.) Live with persons who have Hepatitis B and other chronic liver disease, and 4.) Those who have multiple sex partners.
- Vaccination provides protection for more than 15 years and possibly a lifetime.

BLOODBORNE DISEASES: Case Studies

CASE STUDY #1

Susie cleaned up her sink and counter space at the beauty parlor and called her husband, Joe. While talking with Susie, Joe cleared his desk. They agreed that he would get some milk and eggs from the store on the way home, while Susie stopped to pick up little Joe from kindergarten. “See you soon,” they both said. Susie went to the school to get Little Joe, and Joe Sr. went to the store as planned. He purchased milk and eggs and then stopped by the nearby park for his usual homosexual interlude. When he arrived home, Susie told Joe that there was a strange message from Dr. Brown’s office. Dr. Brown wanted to meet with both of them tomorrow. Joe knew what it was about. He had been tested for HIV two weeks ago, and the results must be in….

---

[2] cdc.gov/hepatitis B enotes.tripod.com/hepatitisB.htm

CASE STUDY #2

They were at the family reunion picnic, and the teenagers were whispering and somber, unlike their usual loud energetic behaviors . . . "Ronnie has AIDS."

Now it's Thanksgiving, the family is gathered around the table, and food is everywhere. A very strong scent overpowers the delicious turkey and dressing and pies. "What is that smell?" "It's bleach. You know Ronnie has AIDS, and we don't want to catch it," whispers a family member.

It's Spring, the birds are singing, and flowers are blooming as the limousine slowly rolls through the winding roads in the cemetery. So many tearful youth, he was only 18, so many *homosexua*l youth. "Where did they come from? What do we do now? Who will be sick next?"

CASE STUDY #3

Paula slowly awoke on the couch after her afternoon nap and knew that it was time to pick up her son from the sitter. She felt just slightly rested, although according to the clock she had slept for two hours. That's the way it's been for the last two years, since she was diagnosed with Hepatitis B. Every day, more than once a day, Paula relives the incident that occurred just before graduation day from Michigan State University. There was a party in the dorm, and an acquaintance had celebrated the last day of school by shooting up heroin. Unknown to Paula, she had Hepatitis B and she dropped the used needle containing her contaminated blood into the trash basket. While cleaning up after the party, Paula pulled the bag of trash from the basket and smashed it down on the floor to compact the contents. The needle punctured her palm, and the blood from it was injected into her hand. Initially, it was just a painful incident, but now in hindsight, she knows that had she just taken the series of three HBV vaccines in her freshman year or even if she had gone to the student health center immediately after the needle stick, she could have had the Immunoglobulin and probably would have avoided having liver damage and certainly would not have passed Hepatitis B to her child during childbirth.

NEEDS OF INDIVIDUALS HAVING BLOODBORNE DISEASES

Once an individual receives medical information of a positive HIV blood test, a series of challenges is presented to the person and his or her family:

- <u>Anger</u> focused on self and partners. Whom to blame? Some take the position that if no one protected me, I will not make an effort to protect anyone else.

- <u>Embarrassment</u> is felt most by the unsuspecting partner.

- <u>All sexual partners</u>, the Health Department and the Center for Disease Control (CDC) must be informed.

- <u>A complete physical exam</u> must be done, including a TB test.

- Medications that prevent infections and slow the speed of destruction of CD4 lymphocyte cells are expensive. There are multiple doses and various kinds of medications, most of which have severe side effects, especially the diarrhea.

- Insurance coverage may or may not be an option for the individual.

- Workdays are missed while going for medical tests and due to the side effects of the medication: Nausea, vomiting, severe gas and diarrhea.

- Financial issues arise due to days missed from work and the cost of medications if not covered by insurance.

- Home environment. There are many complex elements in the home:
  Spouse – Anger, embarrassment, feelings of betrayal, fear of personal illness, how to care for the newly diagnosed person, thoughts of divorce.
  Children – Anger, embarrassment, fear of personal illness.

How to help

- Listen – Allow the individual to vent anger without judging their feelings.

- Confidentiality – Never tell anyone what has been told to you.

- Help with personal forgiveness – Lead the person to Christ and give scriptures to help them find comfort in the Word, as the opportunity presents.

- Refer to the Department of Social Services for financial assistance.

- Encourage participation in and offer transportation if needed to community based AIDS group support sessions for positive individuals, spouses and children.

REALITY CHECK: Believers *should* be the best candidates for donating disease free blood. What an opportunity to save lives both physically and spiritually!!

BLOODBORNE DISEASES ♥ HEALTH & WELLNESS
Prevention & Cleanliness

As long as there is no sexual contact or sharing of blood products or bodily fluids with infected individuals, one is not at risk of getting a bloodborne disease from an infected person. Bodily fluids are semen, vaginal fluids, breast milk, fluid in the uterus and the spinal column.

Recommendations for prevention of bloodborne diseases are:

- Don't share anything that could have an infected person's blood on it, i.e. toothbrushes, razors, nail clippers or body piercing instruments.

- All individuals living in the same household with a Hepatitis B chronically infected individual should be vaccinated against Hepatitis B.

- Clean up any blood spills with household bleach while wearing utility gloves.

- Infected persons should not pre-chew food for babies.

- Cover all sores and rashes and do not touch them to the blood of an infected person.

- Do not share drug needles, cocaine straws or any drug paraphernalia.

Federal health care standards require use of procedures known as Universal Precautions. They give standard methods for safe handling of all bodily fluids, blood and blood products from all individuals in the same safe manner. This is a practice that should be adopted by individuals working in any capacity with the general public, since it significantly reduces the chances of becoming infected with any bloodborne disease.

Cleanliness:

PROPER HAND WASHING TECHNIQUE IS THE MOST IMPORTANT, EASIEST AND LEAST EXPENSIVE WAY TO AVOID VIRAL INFECTIONS AND MOST COMMUNICABLE DISEASES.

<u>The right way to wash your hands:</u>

- Use warm running water and preferably a liquid soap.
- Apply a small quantity of soap to the hands.
- Rub hands together vigorously and ensure soap and water are applied to all surfaces.
- Wash your hands for at least 15 seconds. Suggested sequence: palm to palm, palm over the back of the hand, palm to palm with fingers interlaced, back of the fingers with the opposing palm, rotate rubbing the thumbs in the palm of the hand, rotate again, rubbing the fingers in the palm.
- Rinse hands under running water.
- Leave the water running while drying hands. Dry hands with a clean towel.
- Turn the tap off, preferably touching the fixture with a disposable paper towel.

CHAPTER SUMMARY

BLOOD, LYMPH AND THE WORD:

- Blood contains nutrition, oxygen and cleansing agents needed to maintain life and growth in our physical bodies. Similarly, the Word of God supplies the needs of believers for life, growth and structure in the church.

- Blood is a combination of red cells, white cells and plasma. The Word of God is a combination of Jesus, truth, life and God. By intimately knowing one, we know all.

- Blood and the Word of God offer cleansing, renewal, growth, repair, protection and regulation. Both are preventative in nature, in that they prevent physical and spiritual death and are necessary to maintain life and perpetuate the species.

BLOODBORNE DISEASES – HIV & AIDS

- Bloodborne diseases thrive only in an environment of human blood and are passed person to person when contaminated blood comes in contact with an opening in the skin or the mucous membranes of another person.

- The most common ways the HIV virus is passed are through: 1.) Sexual contact; 2.) Needles shared by substance abusers when injecting drugs; 3.) Needle sticks in health care workers, when the needles contain infected blood; 4.) Females having positive HIV passing it to the fetus during childbirth; and 5.) Infected mothers when nursing infants.

- A diagnosis of positive HIV is destructive to the person, the spouse, children, parents, siblings, friends, the work environment, finances and society as a whole.

- Sooner or later we will all be touched by the realities this disease imposes on someone listed above. Regardless of the level of growth people have attained, the needs listed in Maslow's Hierarchy are important in those who are vulnerable.

- There are safe ways to lend support to infected persons without contracting a blood borne disease.

BLOODBORNE DISEASE – HEPATITIS B

- This disease affects the liver.

- There is a vaccine that prevents contracting the disease.

CLEANLINESS:

- Hand washing is the most important, easiest and least expensive way to avoid infections caused by viruses!

CHAPTER THREE
The Circulatory System

The circulatory system is like an intricate transportation network within the body. Sometimes called the blood vascular system, it consists of the heart and blood vessels.

The overall function of the circulatory system is to keep the blood and lymph moving from one part of the body to another. This movement depends on the circulation of blood within a maze of vessels. The architecture of these vessels is similar to an interstate highway system. Just as a highway system is designed to route vehicles from one destination to another, the vessels of the circulatory system are designed to transport blood to and from various parts of the body. The center of the body's highway system is the heart. This is the pump that maintains circulation in the vessels.

THE HEART IS:

- Situated between the lungs in the chest, with about two thirds of its mass lying to the left of the center of the body. The heart is shaped like a blunt cone about the size of a closed fist.

- A hollow muscular organ that fills with blood and pumps it through the vessels.

- Enclosed in a loose-fitting, two-layered membrane called the pericardium. The inner layer produces a fluid that prevents friction as the heart beats, and the external layer is a tough, fibrous tissue that binds the heart in place in the chest.

- The muscle tissue fibers of the heart are unique in that they contract rapidly, continuously and rhythmically about 72 times a minute, never stopping. Its source of stimulation is a specialized tissue that lies only within the heart. No other muscle in the body has such a source of stimulation and the ability to contract continuously like the heart.

- The specialized tissue in the heart that stimulates contractions can be affected by the nervous system to increase or decrease the heart rate.

- The large vessels carrying blood away from the heart are called arteries. They decrease in size as they get farther away from the heart, branching off in many directions, finally becoming tiny capillaries. At the capillary level nutritional substances are delivered to the cells, and waste substances—carbon dioxide and unneeded chemicals—are picked up in the blood. Vessels called veins then carry the blood back to the lungs and heart..

- So the transport system works, miles of large tubes to those of minute capacity, carrying blood around the body as the heart keeps the system in motion.[1]

THE CIRCULATORY SYSTEM

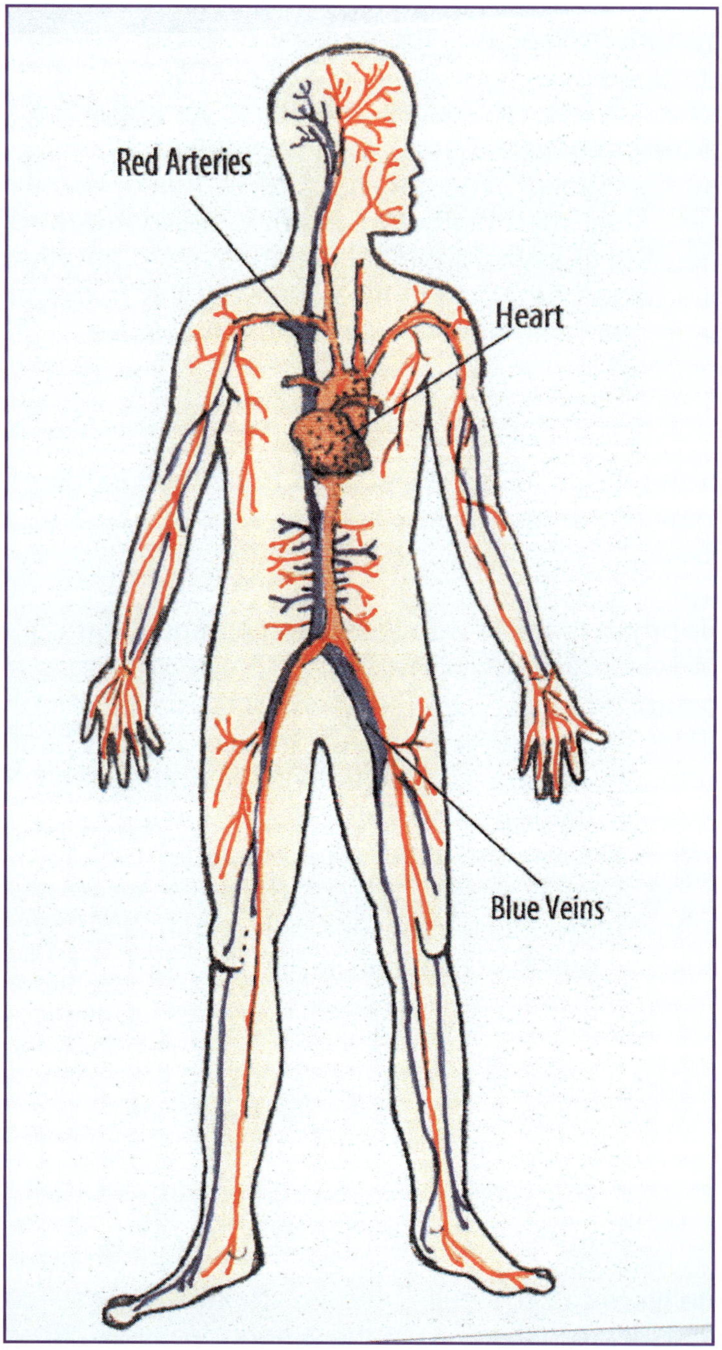

Heart and Blood Vessels

[1] Gerard J. Tortora and Nicholas Anagnosakos, Principles of Anatomy and Physiology (San Francisco: Canfield Press, 1975), pp. 363-367

THE CIRCULATORY SYSTEM: **Pastorate, Clergy and Ministries**

In the Body of Christ, the pastor and spouse are the heart of the church. They provide leadership for the members by setting the spiritual standard and the pace for learning and evangelizing the Word. These are highly accountable positions, just as the heart is in the physical body, because the life of believers and the effectiveness of the Body of Christ on this earth lies in the hands of the pastor. "So thou, O son of man, I have set thee a watchman unto the house of Israel; therefore thou shalt hear the word at my mouth, and warn them from me. When I say unto the wicked, O wicked man, thou shalt surely die; if thou dost not speak to warn the wicked from his way, that wicked man shall die in his iniquity; but his blood will I require at thine hand." (Ezekiel 33:7,8).

God told His people through the prophet Jeremiah, "And I will give you pastors according to mine heart, which shall feed you with knowledge and understanding." (Jeremiah 3:15) God knew that although Christ was the spiritual head of the church, people would need earthly leaders to coordinate their spiritual growth and the spiritual activities and progress of the church. When Paul was in jail and unable to see about the members of the church at Thessalonica where he pastored, he was concerned about their spiritual state and sent Timotheus, a fellow minister, to assess their situation. "... When I could stand it no longer, I sent to find out about your faith. I was afraid that in some way the tempter might have tempted you and our efforts might have been useless." (I Thessalonians 3:5 NIV)

The support staff of clergy and the ministries in the church function like arteries and veins, perpetuating and transporting the Word to the congregation and beyond the walls of the physical church, under the direction of the pastor. "Now ye are the body of Christ, and members in particular. And God hath set some in the church, first apostles, secondarily prophets, thirdly teachers." (I Corinthians 12:27, 28a) The purpose for these functions in the church is to develop members spiritually so that they grow to maturity and fulfill the ministry that Christ has for the church and perfect the Body of Christ. People mature spiritually in cycles, as do cells (see page six).

Knowing humanity, and the potential for them to become arrogant when in positions of power, God instructed Peter to teach ministers proper conduct for their position. "The elders which are among you I exhort, ... Feed the flock of God which is among you, taking the oversight thereof, not by constraint, but willingly; not for filthy lucre, but of a ready mind; ...Neither as being lords over God's heritage, but being ensamples to the flock." (I Peter 5:1a, 2,3) Elders are to be shepherds of God's flock not because they are forced, but willingly; not for money, but eager to serve. Not lording it over the people, but being examples to them.

"Take heed therefore unto yourselves, and to all the flock, over the which the Holy Ghost hath made you overseers, to feed the church of God, which he hath purchased with his own blood." (Acts 20:28). In this passage, Paul was instructing the ministers to check themselves and those to whom they ministered, reminding them that their positions were given by the Holy Ghost and not to use their authority inappropriately. As ministers, they were responsible for feeding *all* of the people, a charge requiring spiritual instruction for people at varied stages of spiritual growth. The fact that God had purchased the church with his own blood makes the flock precious in his sight, and they are not to be misused.

The heart is placed in the chest between the lungs and is protected by the rib cage. The position of pastor is a placement in the church that is protected by God. The Apostle Paul wrote, "And I thank Christ Jesus our Lord, who hath enabled me, for that he counted me faithful, putting me into the ministry." (I Timothy 1:12) Jesus said, "Ye have not chosen me, but I have chosen you, and ordained you that ye should go and bring forth fruit and that your fruit should remain." (John 15:16a) God said, "Touch not mine anointed, and do my prophets no harm." (I Chronicles 16:22)

The heart is a hollow muscular organ that fills with blood. Paul told Timothy, a young minister in the scriptures, "Study to show thyself approved unto God, a workman that needeth not to be ashamed, rightly dividing the word of truth. (II Timothy 2:15) He also told Timothy, "Till I come, give attendance to reading, to exhortation, to doctrine. Meditate on these things; give thyself wholly to them." (I Timothy 4:13 & 15) "O ye Corinthians, our mouth is open unto you, our heart is enlarged." (II Corinthians 6:11) Pastors and ministers must flood their minds with the Word, be filled with the Spirit and their "super sized" hearts must be filled with love for the people of God.

The heart is enclosed in a two-layered membrane called the pericardium. The inner layer prevents friction as the heart beats. This layer represents the pastor's spouse, the intercessor between the congregation and the pastor and to God on behalf of the pastor. The extent of the spouse's participation in the pastor's calling may vary from a public position of assistant pastor to a very private position as friend, lover and emotional supporter. Whatever the level of participation, the spouse of the pastor shares the protection that God gives the pastor. Therefore, the respect given the pastor belongs to the spouse also.

The outer tough fibrous layer of the heart binds it in place in the chest. God's divine protection and security remain with the pastor as long as Jesus is kept in the lead position. Jesus told his disciples, "All power is given unto me in heaven and in earth … and, lo, I am with you alway, even unto the end of the world." (Matthew 28: 18b&20b) God told Jacob when he passed the covenant from his father Isaac to Jacob, "And, behold, I am with thee, and will keep thee in all places whither thou goest, and will bring thee again into this land; *for I will not leave thee, until I have done that which I have spoken to thee of.*" (Genesis 28:15) Pastors have the assurance that God will be with them until they have fully completed the task or assignment God has given.

The heart is made of a special tissue that has a natural inborn rhythm. It beats without nerve stimulation and never gets tired like the muscles of our arms and legs. A pastor is a special kind of person, one who is dedicated beyond the limits of others. Like the TV commercial about the Timex watch from years ago, they can "take-a-licking and keep on ticking". "Therefore seeing we have this ministry, as we have received mercy, we faint not." (II Corinthians 4:1) Paul told the church at Corinth that since it was through God's mercy they had received their ministry, they would neither give in to discouragement nor give up.

There is a special inner motivation, an urgency experienced by a pastor, which is referred to as a "calling." Paul expressed this state, "So, as much as in me is, I am ready to preach the gospel to you that are at Rome also. For I am not ashamed of the gospel of

Christ: for it is the power of God unto salvation to everyone that believeth; to the Jew first, and also to the Greek." (Romans 1:15,16) Jeremiah, an Old Testament prophet, found himself in a position where after giving the people so much bad news from God, a crooked priest had him beaten and put into stocks. Jeremiah got upset with God. He said, "But if I say, 'I will not mention him or speak any more in his name,' his word is in my heart like a fire, a fire shut up in my bones. I am weary of holding it in; indeed, *I cannot*." (Jeremiah 20:9NIV)

The contraction rate of the heart can be changed by nerve stimulation. The inborn rate that the heart beats is 72-80 times per minute. When the need arises, the nervous system causes the heart to increase or decrease the rate. In the spiritual Body of Christ, the Holy Spirit stimulates the pastor, just as the nervous system stimulates the heart in our physical bodies. In both cases the stimulus is given in response to internal or external occurrences. For example, if a snake were placed on a table in front of us, we would have an immediate reaction. One of the reactions to this external occurrence would be a significant increase in the rate and intensity of our heartbeat. Similarly, the pastor under the guidance of the Holy Spirit may vary the rate and intensity of the delivery of the Word or the direction of the ministry of the church, depending on the needs of the congregation or of the community. The Psalmist said, "Where there is no vision, the people perish." (Proverbs 29:18a) The pastor assesses the needs of the congregation and responds in a way that strengthens their knowledge and faith in God. Paul said, "And my speech and my preaching was not with enticing words of man's wisdom, but in demonstration of the Spirit and of power: That your faith should stand not in the wisdom of men, but in the power of God." (I Corinthians 2:4, 5)

The author of the letter to the Hebrews, made a profound observation and decision on behalf of the church he pastored when he said, "Therefore let us leave the elementary teachings about Christ and go on to maturity, not laying again the foundation of repentance from acts that lead to death, and of faith in God, instruction about baptisms, the laying on of hands, the resurrection of the dead, and eternal judgment. *And God permitting, we will do so."* (Hebrews 6:1-3NIV) Enough had been said about Christ's beginnings and enough teaching and preaching about the exciting outward manifestations of the Spirit. Paul decided it was time to teach the Body of Christ about the inward changes that take place with spiritual maturity. It was his responsibility, and with God's help he would do it.

Vessels of various sizes carry blood away from and back to the heart, servicing the cells of the body. Similarly, ministers, apostles, prophets and teachers carry the Word in the spiritual body of Christ. "And he gave some, apostles; and some, prophets; and some, evangelists; and some pastors and teachers: For the perfecting of the saints, for the work of the ministry, for the edifying of the body of Christ." (Ephesians 4:11-12)

Whereas the pastors' preaching gives a steady diet of the Word that establishes a basic and progressive level of spiritual growth for the congregation, evangelists fill the role of motivator. Both Paul and Peter wrote about *stirring up* the readers by "Putting them in remembrance of the things they had been taught and the gift of God that was within." (II Peter 1:13; & II Timothy 1:6) God speaks through evangelists and often performs miracles through them, showing His power. Teaching is a ministry utilized by God, through which

He gives instructions, the *how* to do what was *proclaimed* by preaching. In other words, through preaching we learn about *where* we must be in Christ. Through teaching, we learn the process in step-by-step directions of *how* to get there.

Each level of spreading the Gospel inside and outside the Body of Christ represents a ministry, filling the spiritual needs of individuals. Even the lay person that reaches out a hand to help or encourage another person is a carrier of the gospel, one on one, like the tiniest capillary that carries nutrition and oxygen to the cells.

THE CIRCULATORY SYSTEM ■ PATHOLOGY: **Hypertension (High Blood Pressure)**

The heart squeezes at a normal pressure of 120 mm of mercury when it pumps blood out of its chambers into the lungs and arteries (systolic pressure). When the heart muscle relaxes, the pressure within the heart drops to 80 mm or less of mercury, and blood passively flows into the heart from the body (diastolic pressure). This pressure is read as 120 over 80, (120/80) and is considered normal.

Hypertension is a condition in which the heart squeezes with a force greater than or equal to 140 mm of mercury, and/or has an excess amount of pressure remaining in it , more than 90 mm of mercury, when it is relaxed. This pressure is read as 140 over 90 (140/90). When sustained at this level constantly, the heart does not receive the rest that it needs, resulting in unwanted consequences for the heart, brain, kidneys and eyes.

Causes of Hypertension

Fluid Retention High sodium intake causes the body's cells to retain fluids, which causes increased pressure on the outer surface of blood vessels. The heart must sustain a greater amount of pressure within the vessels to circulate the blood.

Stress Causes the muscles in the arteries to tighten, making the size of the opening in the vessel (lumen) smaller. Then the heart has to squeeze with greater force to move blood through veins and arteries around the body.

Weight Increased body mass increases the amount of fat inside and outside the arteries. Fat puts pressure on the arteries, making it harder for the heart to push blood through. Also, the blood vessels are longer, which again makes the heart pump at a higher pressure to move blood through veins and arteries to the cells of the body.

Consequences of Hypertension

Blindness Occurs due to the high level of pressure on the tiny vessels in the eyes. The vessels eventually break and bleed into the eyes.

Kidney Failure Is a result of the constant pounding of the high-pressured heartbeat, which destroys the tiny vessels in the kidneys, allowing precious electrolytes, vitamins and minerals to leave the body in the urine.

Strokes are the result of the constant, sustained pressure on the arteries in the brain. Sometimes these vessels rupture, causing bleeding into the brain.

Angina When the blood pressure is high, the heart uses more energy to pump the blood. The heart then needs more oxygen to function, and if it cannot meet the demands put on it, the result is chest pain—angina.

Enlarged Heart When the heart uses more than the normal amount of energy to pump blood, the heart muscle enlarges. (Similar to the way the biceps muscle is enlarged in weight lifters). However, since the heart is covered with a fibrous coating that resists stretching, the enlarged muscle of the heart expands inward first, decreasing the amount of blood the heart can hold. Then the heart expands outward into the chest cavity, crowding the lungs. Less blood circulating through an enlarged heart puts even more strain on the heart.

Heart Attacks Are the result of sustained episodes of overwhelming demands on the heart when the heart muscle cannot get enough oxygen. Cells of the heart muscle die due to lack of oxygen. This can result in the heart beating in an irregular rhythm and can lead to varying degrees of heart failure.

THE CIRCULATORY SYSTEM ♥ HEALTH & WELLNESS
Intervention & Prevention

The following behaviors are recommended for people with or without a diagnosis of hypertension:

EAT HEALTHIER - By reducing the amount of fat and sodium in your diet.

REDUCE STRESS LEVELS - By relaxing, walking and managing time.

LOSE WEIGHT – To reduce pressure exerted on the surface of arteries.

TAKE MEDICATIONS AS PRESCRIBED – To help lower your blood pressure and keep it low.

INCREASE ACTIVITY – To strengthen your heart and build more pathways for blood flow to the heart (collateral circulation).

CHAPTER SUMMARY

THE CIRCULATORY SYSTEM FUNCTIONS LIKE THE PASTORATE AND CLERGY:

- The circulatory system is like a transportation network in the body.
- The heart is crucial in the circulatory system as the pastor and spouse are in the church, pumping the substance that is vital to life.
- Clergy and ministries in the church carry the word to people at all levels and capacities, as the blood vessels carry blood throughout the body.
- Pastors and their spouses are placed in the church by God and are protected by him just as the heart is secured in a protected place in the chest.
- The heart is a hollow muscular organ that fills with blood, just as the pastor is filled with the Word of God, by studying, memorizing and obeying the scriptures.
- The heart muscle is made of a special tissue that makes it contract and relax with a steady, continuous rhythm, and it never tires. Pastors are special, in that when the congregation is tired and sleeping, the pastor is studying, planning and praying.
- The Spirit of God gives pastors the vision and sensitivity to regulate the rate and intensity of the delivery of the Word, inside and outside the church. Similarly, the nervous system can change the rate and intensity of the heartbeat, depending on what is happening inside or outside our bodies.
- Even lay people can carry the Word, and when done one on one, this is similar to the blood feeding cells at the capillary level.

HYPERTENSION—HIGH BLOOD PRESSURE

- Hypertension is a sustained blood pressure over 140/90.
- The heart beating at a high pressure causes damage to the tiny vessels of the eyes leading to blindness; it damages the tiny vessels of the kidneys, leading to kidney failure; and damages tiny vessels of the brain, leading to strokes. This high pressure also causes damage to the vessels of the heart and can cause an enlarged heart, angina and heart attacks.
- <u>Hypertension can be controlled</u>.

CHAPTER FOUR
The Digestive System

The function of the digestive system is to prepare food for consumption by the cells. The organs of the digestive system are: the mouth, pharynx, esophagus, stomach, small intestines and large intestines. Auxiliary organs of this system are the pancreas, liver and gall bladder.

The nutritional substance in most food we eat is too large to pass through the plasma membranes of the cells. Therefore, chemical and mechanical digestion must occur to break it down into vitamins, minerals, electrolytes, amino acids etc., particles small enough to pass through the walls of the digestive system and ultimately into the cells of our bodies.

Five basic activities of digestion are:

1) **Ingestion** is eating, taking food into the body. The teeth pulverize (chew) the food and mix it with saliva so that it can be swallowed. The saliva begins the chemical digestion of food.

2) **Peristalsis** is movement of food along the digestive tract, similar to the muscular movements of a snake. Once swallowed, food moves into the stomach, which is originally the size of a large sausage. The stomach stretches immeasurably to accommodate its contents. Emotions such as anger, fear and anxiety may slow digestion.

   The pancreas adds digestive enzymes and insulin to the intestines.

   The liver makes heparin, gets rid of worn out red blood cells and bacteria, breaks down poisons in the body and stores those that the body cannot discharge. It changes sugar to fat, stores the fat and changes it back to sugar when needed for energy. The liver also stores vitamins.

   The gall bladder stores bile that is made in the liver. It is used to break down fat.

3) **Mechanical and chemical digestion** takes place from the mouth down through the small intestines. Mechanical digestion involves chewing and the automatic squeezing and sloshing around of the food in the digestive tract. Chemical digestion takes place when acids, enzymes and bacteria are released into the digestive tract to break down the foods. Together, these processes change food into forms that can be used by the cells.

4) **Absorption** is the passage of nutrients from the digestive system into the blood and then to the cells.

5) **Elimination** is the process of releasing undigestible substances from the body.[1]

THE DIGESTIVE SYSTEM

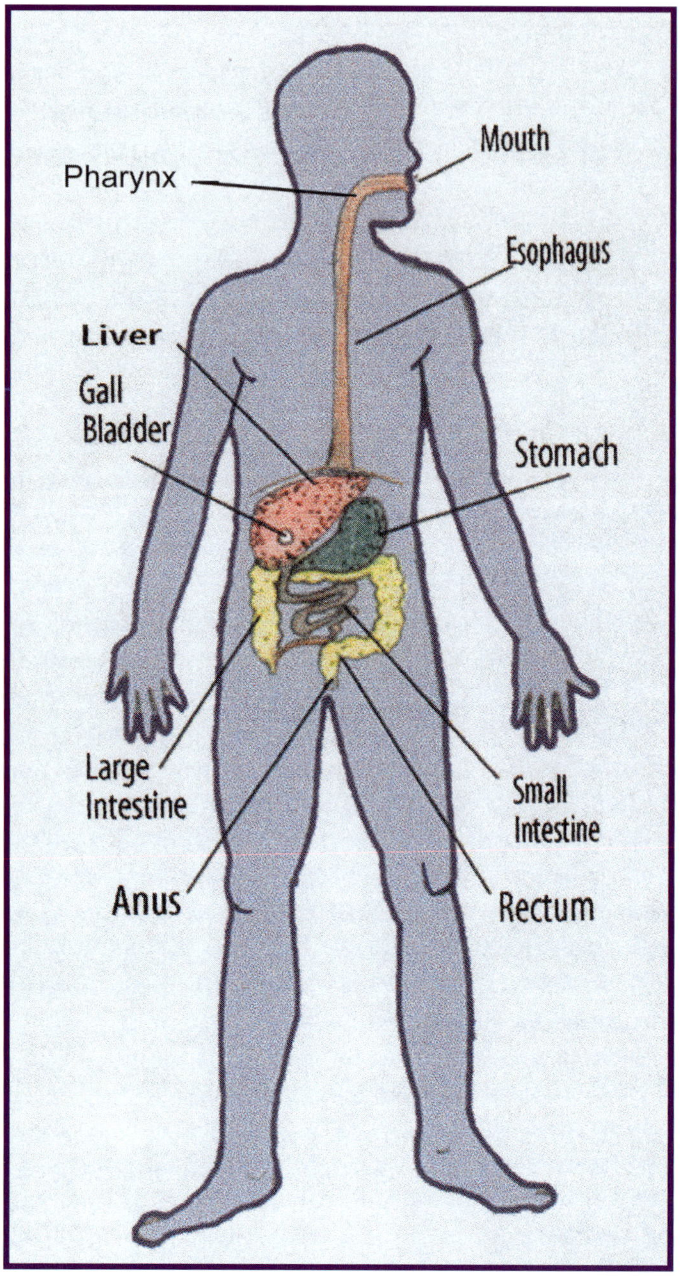

Mouth, Pharynx, Esophagus, Stomach, Small Intestine Large Intestine
Auxiliary Organs: Liver, Gall Bladder (Pancreas pg. 96)

[1] Gerard J. Tortora and Nicholas Anagnostakos, Principles of Anatomy and Physiology (San Francisco: Canfield Press, 1975), pp.457-485

DIGESTIVE SYSTEM: **Digesting the Word**

The Word of God is the spiritual food for believers and those on the path to becoming "born again" individuals. Its spiritual and emotional merits for our existence have already been examined. The Word we also believe comes to us through pastors, ministers and ministries, chosen and anointed by God. Digestion is the most important step in the process of physical, emotional and spiritual growth. No matter how nutritious a sermon or testimony may be, or how interesting or well presented it is, if it is not believed and incorporated into the life of the hearer, it serves no purpose for personal or spiritual development. The Bible tells us in the book of James, "But be ye doers of the word, and not hearers only." (James 1:22a) The same principle holds true regarding food for our natural bodies in that it must be eaten and digested to maintain life and development. Being around it, smelling and handling it adds no nutritional value to our bodies.

Psychologically, everything that enters the consciousness through our senses feeds the mind and spirit. In this information age of high technology we utilize the television, radio, cell phones, faxes, interactive videos etc. to exchange data day and night. This ingestion, this conscious assimilation of sensory data by the five senses—sight, hearing, touch, smell and taste--influences and stimulates us. Then, thought-by-thought and case-by-case, we decide what will be kept in the mind for meditation and thus digested and what will be rejected, sloughed off and forgotten.

Information that is most easily retained in our memory includes the visualizations and experiences that appeal to the senses and those that are frequently repeated. The psyche is most attracted to things or ideas that require little or no effort to discipline the mind or body. Sensory information of that type results in effortless learning and has the potential to lure individuals into a meaningless, stagnant life. Initiating change requires going against the grain of peers, an effort to focus, a purpose and a sense of direction.

Similarly, there are substances that we eat such as salt and sugars, which require minimal digestion by the body because they are quickly and easily absorbed through the gums and cheeks inside the mouth. These substances have nutritional value when taken in regulated quantities, but under some circumstances they can create life-threatening consequences when taken in excess. Also, there are additives and preservatives in certain foods that have no nutritional value and in fact have long-term negative consequences for the body. Most fast foods and commercially prepared frozen and canned entrees fit this category. We are attracted to them because they are quick and easy to obtain, but they are not the selections that promote our health and wellness.

The digestive system must process foods so that the body's cells can use the nutrition from meats, complex carbohydrates, fruits and vegetables. Such foods provide the essential nourishment the body needs to sustain physical growth and to maintain a constant state of wellness. The same is true for spiritual and psychological nourishment for growth and wellness, which comes from the Word of God, educational systems, personal reading, experience and practice. The digestive process for the mind and spirit requires thought, meditation, practice, change and the assimilation of sound principles into one's way of life.

Ingestion *is eating , taking food into the body.* This is an active process in which a decision is made with every bite to digest the food by chewing it or to reject it by spitting it out. Decisions made about food include what to eat, when to eat, how much and where to eat, depending on the taste and texture of the food to be eaten and the degree of hunger. The decision is made based on predetermined standards due to the culture and conditioning of the individual.

Wisdom and sound judgment about the appropriate food to allow into our bodies and the subject matter to allow in our minds are indispensable for our physical, spiritual and psychological state of health. In life we train ourselves to certain principles; then we become what the principles have taught us. When we are disciplined and eat the proper foods, we become physically strong and healthy, and when we learn and practice the truths of the Bible, we develop wholesome habits with strong moral and spiritual character.

The information taken into our minds must be balanced, predetermined and focused. To reach a higher level of maturity, prosperity or productivity one must utilize his/her God-given ability to intelligently evaluate information from the environment as it comes streaming into his or her consciousness, as to its potential for good or for ill. Otherwise, our minds and spirits will dwell on and absorb the information that comes with the least amount of effort and give minimal or no value to life. With physical digestion, we decide what to eat or what to spit out, depending on likes and dislikes.

To the born again and those seeking salvation, the psalmist once said, "O taste and see that the Lord is good: blessed (happy) is the man that trusteth in him." (Psalm 34:8) In this context, taste means to experience. In the midst of today's age of technology, the Psalmist would say that although information is coming toward you from many directions and much of it is worthy, experience a small taste of God's Word and you will find that the Lord is good. Those who trust in Him continuously are happy. Taste may be sweet or bitter, spicy or bland. Each taste or experience of life in light of the Word of God adds depth and value to the soul and spirit.

***Peristalsis** is the movement of food along the digestive tract.* As food moves along the digestive tract, the capacity of the stomach enlarges, and auxiliary organs (liver, gall bladder and pancreas) introduce products that enhance digestion. At this stage, a person has taken food into the mouth, chewed and swallowed it. A decision has been made to physically digest the morsel and accept the outcome of continuous health or eventual illness.

Spiritually and psychologically, information that is retained, mulled over (digested) in the mind is the essence of what a person becomes. "For as he thinketh in his heart, so is he:" (Proverbs 23:7a). Paul challenged the people at the church in Philippi to predetermine certain themes for thought: "Finally, brethren, whatsoever things are true, whatsoever things are honest, whatsoever things are just, whatsoever things are pure, whatsoever things are lovely, whatsoever things are of good report; if there be any virtue, and if there be any praise, think on these things." (Philippians 4:8)

In the Old Testament, God's chosen people lost their focus on God and became all mixed up with the gods and customs of other nations. They were wicked, and God was angry with them. While talking with the prophet Isaiah, God said to tell the people: "Hear ye indeed, but understand not; and see ye indeed, but perceive not. Make the heart of this people fat, and make their ears heavy, and shut their eyes; *Otherwise, they might see with their eyes, and hear with their ears, and understand with their heart and turn and be healed.* (Isaiah 6:9KJV,10NIV)

God allowed the Israelites to defeat themselves by hearing and seeing what was happening around them without understanding (digesting) what was going on. Their hearts (minds) took in *everything* and were overcome with fat, making them calloused and careless, causing them to defeat themselves. Had they just listened to the words from God, digested the information that they saw and heard as God worked on their behalf and allowed digestive enzymes of love and faith to change their minds, they would have understood with their hearts, turned their lives around and would have been *healed*. The same principle holds true in the world today. "Jesus Christ the same yesterday, and today, and for ever." (Hebrews 13:8)

***Mechanical digestion** is the chewing that took place in the mouth.* The squeezing of food swallowed as it moves it along the system is called mechanical digestion. Once food is broken down further to a microscopic size by the enzymes and acids in the intestines, it can be absorbed into the cells. This process is called **chemical digestion**.

Spiritual digestion of the Word (the counterpart of chemical digestion of food) takes place when we meditate on the word of God, which interacts with and is transfigured by faith. "But the word preached did not profit them, not being mixed with faith in them that heard it." (Hebrews 4:2b). The writer wanted the church to know that faith is very important to digesting the Word and when the Word and faith are taken in the optimal combination, the believer's need is satisfied and he/she profits from it. The prophet Jeremiah found solace in God's Word during a time when he was being persecuted. He said, "Thy words were found, and I did eat them; and thy Word was unto me the joy and rejoicing of mine heart." (Jeremiah 15:16) God's Word produces various by-products within us. For Jeremiah, in this instance, it was *joy*.

***Absorption** takes place once food has been chemically broken down to its smallest size.* When food is in nutritional units of vitamins, electrolytes (sodium and potassium) and fluids, then the cells of the body can absorb them and grow, mature and reproduce.

Jesus told his disciples, "If ye continue in my word, then are ye my disciples indeed." (John 8:31b) By maintaining continuous intake and meditation on the Word, we become true followers of Jesus, perpetuating the ministry that he started while on this earth.

Insulin, produced by the pancreas, travels to the cells of the body and surrounds them. When glucose (a form of sugar that comes from food and is necessary for the life of the cells) gets to the cells, insulin makes the cells capable of absorbing the glucose. The cells then use the glucose for energy to grow and respond to the surrounding environment.

The Word, absorbed into the heart and mind, produces an interesting thought or concept. Belief is the insulin in our spiritual lives, because it internalizes the thought or concept, causing one to act on the Word and thus assimilate it into life's day-to-day decisions and priorities. It energizes us to follow through and not give up. The Psalmist said, "I had fainted (quit), unless I had *believed* to see the goodness of the Lord in the land of the living." (Psalm 27:13).

The stomach was described as the size of a large sausage, capable of stretching *immeasurably* to accommodate its contents. Believers must acquire a desire to learn the

Word and grow to deeper levels than just "Jesus loves me". Peter told the believers, "As newborn babes, desire the sincere milk of the word, that ye may grow thereby." (I Peter 2:2). That was in the beginning of their walk with God. In Hebrews, the writer prodded the believers to attain an even deeper knowledge of the scriptures. "Anyone who lives on milk, being still an infant, is not acquainted with the teaching about righteousness. But solid food is for the mature, who by constant use have trained themselves to distinguish good from evil." (Hebrews 5:13-14NIV) The wisdom (knowledge of God) conveyed in the Gospel of Christ causes growth toward excellence in righteousness, resulting in maturity and experience in distinguishing right from wrong. Believers are encouraged to reach the level of transcendence—the point when one knows the way and can be a witness and give assistance to others—to help them grow. One's capacity for spiritual knowledge is immeasurable, like the increasing size of the stomach.

Elimination is the process of releasing undigestible substances from the body. The process of growth requires eliminating waste and toxins from the body. Non value-added habits, beliefs, expenses, expenditures of time, foods etc. must be eliminated and replaced with value-added habits, beliefs etc. The writer of Hebrews told the believers, "Let us lay aside every weight, and the sin which doth so easily beset us, and let us run with patience the race that is set before us." (Hebrews 12:1b) Like an athlete who gets rid of any extras that may hinder his/her performance in the race, so we must prepare ourselves for this life. It is also important to maintain focus while eliminating waste. Paul said, "Brethren, I count not myself to have apprehended: but this one thing I do, forgetting those things which are behind, and reaching forth unto those things which are before, I press toward the mark for the prize of the high calling of God in Christ Jesus." (Philippians 3:13-14)

Digestion is a process that occurs inside a person. Yet the evidence of the balance of the natural and/or spiritual diet shows outwardly to the world via our appearance and way of life. Jesus said, "Let your light so shine before men, that they may see your good works, and glorify your father which is in heaven." (Matthew 5:16) When spiritual digestion takes place, believers *know* their position and are able to w*ork* their position in the Body of Christ. "And ye are complete in him, which is the head of all principality and power." (Colossians 2:10)

REALITY CHECK:

When was the last time you changed your opinion, your direction, or your priorities because of something you read in the Bible or heard from a messenger of the Lord?

Diabetes Mellitus

Diabetes Mellitus is a disease in which the body either does not produce or does not properly use insulin, a hormone that is needed to convert sugar, starches and other food into energy needed for daily life. The cause of diabetes is a mystery, although both genetics and environmental factors such as obesity and lack of exercise appear to play roles. There are two major types of diabetes.[2]

Type 1 — An autoimmune disease in which the body does not produce insulin. It occurs most often in children and young adults. People with type 1 diabetes must take daily insulin injections to stay alive.

Type 2 — A metabolic disorder resulting from the body's inability to make enough, or properly use, insulin. It is the most common form of the disease, accounting for 90-95 percent of diabetes. Type 2 diabetes is nearing epidemic proportions, because of an increasing number of older Americans and a greater prevalence of obesity and sedentary lifestyles. These people often have no symptoms.

People who are at greatest risk for Type 2 diabetes are:

- ✓ Over age 45
- ✓ Those with a family history of diabetes
- ✓ Those who are overweight
- ✓ Those who do not exercise regularly
- ✓ Those who have low HDL (good) cholesterol or high triglycerides
- ✓ Some ethnic groups (e.g. African Americans, Asian Americans, Pacific Islanders, Hispanics/Latinos and American Indians)
- ✓ Women who had gestational diabetes, a form of diabetes occurring in 2-5 percent of all pregnancies, or who have had a baby weighing 9 pounds or more at birth.

Warning Signs of Diabetes

Type 1 Diabetes	**Type 2 Diabetes**
• Frequent urination • Unusual thirst • Unusual weight loss	• Any of the type 1 symptoms • Blurred vision • Recurring skin, gum, yeast or bladder infections

Table 2. Diabetes Type1, Type 2

[2] John Hopkins University, Michael J. Klag John Hopkins Family Health Book First Edition (New York: Harper Collins 1999), pp. 1174-1179

Complications of Diabetes:

Blindness
Is caused when the tiny blood vessels in the eyes become fragile and bleed (retinopathy). This can also lead to retinal detachment. Diabetics may also experience pressure in the eyes (glaucoma) and clouding of the eye's lens (cataracts). Diabetes is the leading cause of new cases of blindness in people ages 20-74. Each year, up to 24,000 people lose their sight because of diabetes.

Kidney Disease
Is caused when there is thickening of the walls of the membrane that strains the urine in the kidney. This causes kidneys to stop cleaning waste from the blood. Diabetes is the leading cause of end-stage kidney failure.

Nerve Disease and Amputations
Damage to tiny nerves and blood vessels in the feet and legs leads to infections and amputations. People with diabetes may have nerve damage, which, if severe, can lead to lower limb amputations.

High Blood Pressure
Is caused when plaque and fatty tissues accumulate in the capillaries, veins and arteries, making the opening for blood flow smaller. The heart must then pump with greater force to move blood to the cells

Heart Disease
Is caused when the arteries become brittle and the heart must pump more forcefully, leading to hypertension.

Strokes
Added pressure on the arteries of the brain may cause bleeding into the brain, known as a stroke.

Diabetes Intervention/Prevention

IF YOU HAVE ALREADY BEEN DIAGNOSED WITH DIABETES:

- Follow the diet recommended by your physician.
- Take prescribed medications as ordered by your physician.
- Schedule and go for routine check-ups as directed by your physician.
- Try to maintain your blood sugar within the recommended limits. This will help you minimize complications such as damage to your nerves, kidneys, blood vessels and eyes caused by high blood sugar; and the risk of confusion and loss of consciousness due to low blood sugar.
- Ask your doctor to do a glycohemoglobin (HbA1c) test at least twice per year. This test shows your blood sugar level averaged over a three-month period, which helps the doctor better determine your adherence and response to diabetic therapy.[3]

IF YOU ARE DIABETIC OR IN THE "AT RISK" CATEGORY:

- Exercise daily.
- Maintain your weight.
- Eat a proper diet.
- Reduce your fat intake.
- Get annual physical check-ups.

[3] John Hopkins University, Michael J. Klag Johns Hopkins Family Health Book First Edition (New York: Harper Collins, 1999), pp. 1176,1178

CHAPTER SUMMARY

THE DIGESTIVE SYSTEM AND DIGESTING THE WORD:

- Psychologically, everything that enters consciousness via our senses on a daily basis feeds the mind and spirit.

- Simple sugars, sodium and water are quickly and easily absorbed by the body, as is information that requires the least amount of discipline of the mind or body.

- Ingestion involves a decision we make as to what food or information to take in. It requires wisdom and discipline to make choices that will be most beneficial to the body, mind and spirit.

- Peristalsis is the movement of food along the digestive tract, similar to the process of thinking about or mulling over information.

- Chemical digestion occurs when enzymes and acids in the intestines break down food. Spiritual digestion takes place through meditating on the Word and mixing it with faith and belief.

- Absorption takes place in the cells once the food is broken down into the form of vitamins and electrolytes etc. When the Word is absorbed into the mind and spirit and mixed with belief, it causes growth and change in the individual.

- Elimination involves the release of undigestible substances from the body, as well as non value-added practices from our lives.

- A balanced or unbalanced natural and/or spiritual diet is evident to the world by our way of life.

DIABETES MELLITUS

- Is a condition in which the body does not produce or does not properly use insulin.

- Chances for complications of diabetes decrease when blood sugar is maintained at the recommended level.

- A reduced fat diet and exercise are important behaviors for those with diabetes and those in the at risk category.

- Complications of diabetes include blindness, kidney disease, amputations, heart disease, stroke and high blood pressure.

CHAPTER FIVE
The Skeletal System

The skeletal system forms the framework of the body and consists of approximately 206 bones.

- The way our bodies function in daily life—moving about and manipulating objects physically—depends on the integrity of the skeletal system and muscles.

Functions of the bones:

- Bones provide a framework of support for the body.
- Bones have spots strategically placed for muscle attachment so that they can give leverage to muscles, allowing movement of the body.
- Red blood cells are produced in the marrow of bones.
- Bones store minerals such as calcium, phosphates, carbonate and magnesium.

Bones are arranged in the body to protect and enhance the function of underlying organs:

- Bones of the skull protect the brain.
- Pelvic bones protect the reproductive and urinary organs.
- The bones of the rib cage are specially shaped and positioned to protect the heart and lungs, allowing the lungs to expand and relax while breathing.

Joints

The term articulation or joint refers to a point of contact between bones or between cartilage and bones. The structure of a joint determines its function.

All movements of the body that change its position take place at the joints.

Since bones are much too rigid to bend, the skeletal system consists of many separate bones, which are held together at the joints by flexible connective tissue.[1]

---

[1] Gerard J. Tortora and Nicholas Anagnostakos, Principles of Anatomy and Physiology (San Francisco: Canfield Press, 1975), pp.111-158

THE SKELETAL SYSTEM

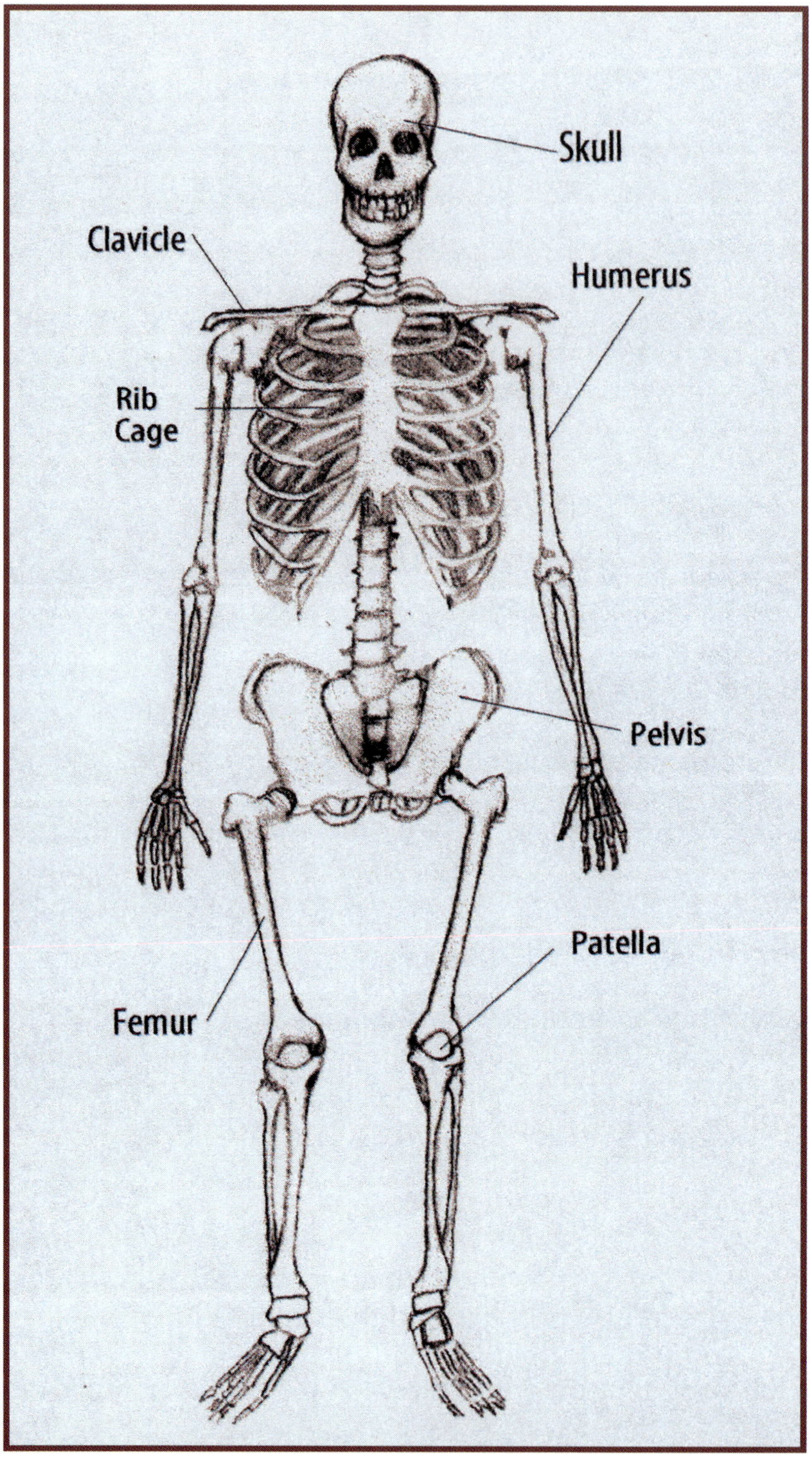

Bones and Joints

THE SKELETAL SYSTEM **Church Leadership and Structure**

The Spirit of Christ resides in believers, who make up the Body of Christ, the spiritual church. When there are more than two people united by a common bond, there must be a system of order, a framework, chain of command that maintains the structure of the group so that their common interests can be served. Those who are in positions of leadership in the physical church form the framework that houses the spiritual church, where the Spirit of Christ resides. The bones of the skeletal system form the framework of our physical body where our mind and spirit live. The common bond in the spiritual Body of Christ is the Spirit of Christ, which comes from God, and the common interest of the members is to fulfill God's purpose on this earth. With the growth in membership of the New Testament Body of Christ, caring for the needs of members became more complex. To accommodate the needs of individual members in addition to the financial and business concerns of the church, the disciples initiated leadership positions under the guidance of the Holy Spirit. This allowed the disciples to freely concentrate on the spiritual needs and spiritual growth of the believers.

"In those days when the number of disciples was increasing, the Grecian Jews among them complained against the Hebraic Jews because their widows were being overlooked in the daily distribution of food. So the Twelve gathered all the disciples together and said, 'It would not be right for us to neglect the ministry of the word of God in order to wait on tables. Brothers, choose seven men from among you who are known to be full of the Spirit and wisdom. We will turn this responsibility (business) over to them and will give our attention to prayer and the ministry of the word." (Acts 6:1-4 NIV)

In one of the apostle Paul's analogies, he described the church as a building, emphasizing its complex structure and strength, noting that it has a firm foundation and cornerstone, grows as bricks are added to the building and is the dwelling place for God's Spirit. "And are built upon the foundation of the apostles and prophets, Jesus Christ himself being the chief corner stone; In whom all the building fitly framed together groweth unto an holy temple in the Lord: In whom ye also are builded together for an habitation of God through the Spirit." (Ephesians 2:20-22) The Spirit of God dwells comfortably within the spiritual Body of Christ when there is structure, order and respect in the membership. The members realize that Christ is the foundation—the purpose for the organization—and they are the bricks that form the dwelling place for the presence of God. Members form the visible Body of Christ that is viewed by the world, and church leaders are in the forefront. Church leaders are akin to the skeleton of the body in that they comprise the framework of the church, giving it structure and form.

Our minds and spirits live in our bodies, which are framed and supported by a skeleton made of bones. Our skeletons are subject to—obedient to—our minds, fulfilling the purpose of the mind. Our minds obey our spirit, which connects with God's spirit when we have been *quickened*. Then, as the Word of God is preached and taught to believers, they digest the Word and grow to maturity. As believers interact with, influence and pray for people, the people develop a respect for the cause of Christ and a desire to experience similar beliefs and benefits in their lives. "And they, continuing daily with one accord in the temple, and breaking bread from house to house, did eat their meat with gladness and singleness of heart, praising God, and having favour with all the people. And the Lord added to the church daily such as should be saved." (Acts 2:46-47) Cells and believers, producing more cells and believers, result in growth of the physical and spiritual body.

The way we function in daily life--move about and manipulate objects physically—depends on the INTEGRITY of the skeletal system and muscles. The integrity of bones refers to strength, completeness and unbroken-ness. Integrity for one in a leadership position is defined as steadfast adherence to a strict ethical code; honesty.[2]

A leader is one who is in charge or in command of others.[3] One who executes assigned duties. The foremost spiritual leader recognized in a church organization is accountable directly to Christ in carrying out His vision and mission through the church. All staff in the church's chain of command are accountable to the leader and to Christ when they are carrying out the leaders' vision for the church. The qualities for the leading positions of the church were given in the Bible because the reputation and effectiveness of the church in the community depend on the moral and spiritual integrity of its leaders. When leaders with integrity represent the church, it is a solid and strong organization, free of embarrassment.

The apostle Paul described the qualifications of two positions of leadership in the church, that of bishop and that of deacon. In the first category (that of bishop) this writer will include the ministers/clergy of the church. "Now the overseer (bishop) must be above reproach, the husband of but one wife, temperate, self-controlled, respectable, hospitable, able to teach, not given to drunkenness, not violent but gentle, not quarrelsome, not a lover of money. He must manage his own family well and see that his children obey him with proper respect. (If anyone does not know how to manage his own family, how can he take care of God's church?) He must not be a recent convert, or he may become conceited and fall under the same judgment as the devil. He must also have a good reputation with outsiders, so that he will not fall into disgrace and into the devil's trap." (I Timothy 3:2-7 NIV)

In the apostle Paul's second category of leaders (that of deacon), the writer will include all who hold offices in the church, other than the ministers/clergy. "Deacons, likewise, are to be men worthy of respect, sincere, not indulging in much wine, and not pursuing dishonest gain. They must keep hold of the deep truths of the faith with a clear conscience. They must first be tested; and then if there is nothing against them, let them serve as deacons. In the same way, their wives are to be women worthy of respect, not malicious talkers but temperate and trustworthy in everything. A deacon must be the husband of but one wife and must manage his children and his household well." (I Timothy 3:8-12NIV)

Bones support the body. Deacons support the church when they monitor and oversee maintenance of the church building, its contents and the financial business of the church. The magnitude of this position is the wisdom, faith and spiritual insight required to responsibly manage the tithes and offerings believers give to God. "And all the tithe of the land, whether of the seed of the land, or of the fruit of the tree, is the Lord's: It is holy unto the Lord." (Leviticus 27:30) There is a balance to be kept between expenditures for the physical church, the pastor and outreach ministries. This requires spiritual insight and

---

[2] *American Heritage College Dictionary* Third Edition (Boston, New York: Houghton Mifflin, 1997)
[3] Ibid.

guidance. "At the end of three years thou shalt bring forth all the tithe of thine increase … And the Levite, (because he hath no part nor inheritance with thee,) and the stranger, and the fatherless, and the widow, which are within thy gates, shall come and shall eat and be satisfied; that the Lord thy God may bless thee in all the work of thine hand which thou doest." (Deuteronomy 14:28-29)

All leaders represent the church and gospel of Christ as they move about in the community. They, like the bones of our bodies, can support the church only if they lead lives of integrity. A fractured bone in a leg has lost its integrity. It cannot support the weight of the body.

Bones provide points of attachment for muscles and give leverage to muscles to allow movement . The leverage that deacons apply is in budgeting financial resources for ministries to operate within and without the walls of the church. The church is then blessed via the tithes and offerings of the membership and the fruit of its ministries. "Cast thy bread upon the waters: for thou shalt find it after many days." (Ecclesiastes 11:1) Church leaders provide training, direction and support for the ministries of the church so that they can have a positive effect inside and beyond the walls of the church. Knowledge, a purpose and a mission are effective tools to leverage against the forces of evil.

Red blood cells are produced in the marrow of bones. Leaders of all ministries in the church should have experience and sound knowledge of the Word of God—like red blood cells in the bones—and should be capable of teaching others. Stephen, one of the seven deacons chosen in the early church, became an outstanding witness for God. "And Stephen, full of faith and power, did great wonders and miracles among the people. And they were not able to resist the wisdom and the spirit by which he spake." (Acts 6:8,10)

Bones store minerals such as calcium, phosphates, carbonate and magnesium. Minerals make bones strong. When needed by the cells of the body, they are available. One of the characteristics the disciples looked for in the candidates for deacons was wisdom, a requirement of the Body of Christ as much as minerals are for the physical body. Wisdom requires experience in life's hardships as well as in spiritual matters so that one is able to advise and give direction to others. This is a quality that comes with study and maturity. "Study to show thyself approved unto God, a workman that needeth not to be ashamed, rightly dividing the word of truth." (II Timothy 2:15) "But the wisdom that is from above is first pure, then peaceable, gentle, and easy to be entreated, full of mercy and good fruits, without partiality, and without hypocrisy." (James 3:17) Maslow's Hierarchy of human needs reinforces this view. The true spiritual leader must have attained at least the level of maturity where they are emotionally and spiritually secure to be able to look after the needs of others.

Bones are arranged in the body to protect and enhance the function of underlying organs.

- Bones of the skull protect the brain. Spiritually, the head of the church is Christ. Church leaders must protect the integrity of the gospel, keeping it as the guide for all decisions and actions taken on behalf of the church. Paul wrote that he was "Set for the defense of the gospel." (Philippians 1:17)

- Pelvic bones protect the reproductive system. Spiritually, the reproductive system of the church involves young children, potential believers and the newly born believers. Leaders must include them as much as possible in activities that stimulate learning and growth. "But Jesus said, suffer little children, and forbid them not, to come unto me: for of such is the kingdom of heaven." (Matthew 19:14)

- The bones of the rib cage protect the heart and lungs. In this book of parallels, the pastor and wife represent the heart in the Body of Christ. The lungs (Chapter Eleven) symbolize prayer. All levels of leadership are in place to protect the pastor and wife through prayer. Paul requested that the Ephesian church pray for all saints, "And for me, that utterance may be given unto me, that I may open my mouth boldly, to make known the mystery of the gospel." (Ephesians 6:19) Leaders should be able to solve *some* problems that occur in the congregation before they reach the pastor. This conserves the pastor's concentration for the spiritual needs of the congregation. *Especially on Sunday mornings!!*

The point of contact where bones articulate (come together) is called a joint. Leaders must be able to work within their groups and with others at higher or lower levels of responsibility. They must also be able to articulate with the world outside the church walls, being capable and full of faith.

An effective living church has levels of leadership. All levels of leadership share the responsibility for the spirituality of the church and its members. It is important that leaders of all ministries of the church understand the responsibilities inherent in their organizational position and understand and support the pastor's vision for that ministry. Structure is more than holding a leadership position; it is people in positions knowing their roles and responsibilities and working with the team to achieve them. This spiritual unity and focus on the ministry promote progress and prevent the church from becoming a political or social group caught in the grips of the world without contact with the living Word. Dissonance between leaders when absent the Holy Spirit leads to spiritual stagnation of the members and an apathetic body.

All movements of the body that change its position take place at the joints. Church leaders must work together (articulate) to move the church into the community. Knowing the purpose and mission of the group that they lead, having lines of demarcation for their positions and expectations for results are vital to the success of the organization. These leaders assist members to attain goals and facilitate overcoming differences among themselves by focusing on the big picture, Christ's mission for the church. Sound organizational structure promotes personal and spiritual growth, which enhances growth of the organization. Without these essential elements, an organization is handicapped, like a physical body without the skeletal structure of bones and joints.

Bones are held together at the joints by flexible connective tissue. In the spiritual church, love is the connective tissue that holds leaders together. "Speaking the truth in love, we will in all things grow up into him who is the Head, that is, Christ. From him the whole body, joined and held together by every supporting ligament, grows and builds itself up in love, as each part does its work." (Ephesians 4:15-16NIV)

Visualizing the church as the Body of Christ makes it alive to believers, and as Jesus' bride, the church is as precious to him as his own body. One day Christ will present the church to God the father and for this purpose, he has prepared a place. Jesus told his disciples, "In my Father's house are many mansions: if it were not so, I would have told you. I go to prepare a place for you." (John 14:2) On the Isle of Patmos, John wrote, "And I John saw the holy city, New Jerusalem, coming down from God out of heaven, prepared as a bride adorned for her husband." (Revelations 21: 2)

THE SKELETAL SYSTEM ■ PATHOLOGY
Osteoarthritis and Rheumatoid Arthritis

The ends of bones are covered with cartilage, a smooth, resilient tissue that cushions the impact of body weight while walking and running. A membrane (synovial membrane) covers the joint space and produces fluid to lubricate the joint. A fibrous protective capsule surrounds the membrane, and bands of fibrous tissues called ligaments bind all of the parts of the joint together.

The problems that occur in the joints due to mechanical failure of the parts are called osteoarthritis (wear-and-tear arthritis). Joint disorders attributed to inflammation produced by infection, disease or some unknown cause are called rheumatoid arthritis.

OSTEOARTHRITIS

Signs and symptoms of osteoarthritis are pain in a joint during or after use, discomfort in a joint before or during a change in the weather, swelling and a loss of flexibility in a joint, bony lumps on the end and middle joints of the fingers.

The degenerating process of a joint affected by osteoarthritis begins with a gradual deterioration of the cartilage. The cartilage loses its cushioning effect, and the shiny smooth surface gets rough. Eventually, the ends of the bones are affected, as bony tissues grow along the sides of the bone (bone spurs), and produce lumps. This is a painful, degenerating process and commonly occurs in the neck, back, knee or hip.

Wear and tear is a principal cause of osteoarthritis, which is sometimes called degenerative joint disease. Athletes who sustain joint injuries and laborers whose joints are stressed daily by the physical demands of the job are at heightened risk of developing arthritic joints later in life.

A diagnosis of osteoarthritis is based on the presence of pain in either one or several joints, bony lumps on the joints of the fingers (women have them about 10 times as often as men), bone spurs evident on X-ray of the joint and blood tests that exclude other types of arthritis. Elderly people are more likely to have osteoarthritis than young people, and it doesn't go away.[4]

Treatment of this joint disease includes exercise focused on range of motion for the joints and muscle strengthening. Various types of heat therapies may be recommended by your physician. Weight control is important to relieve unnecessary pressure on the joints along with practice of good posture. You may also need medication such as aspirin or other anti-inflammatory drugs, or acetaminophen and injections of corticosteroid drugs.

---

[4] David E. Larson, M.D. Mayo Clinic Family Health Book Second Edition (New York: William Morrow and Company Inc., 1996), pp. 907-911

Surgical hip or knee replacement may be advised after long-term joint deterioration has occurred.

RHEUMATOID ARTHRITIS

Rheumatoid arthritis is thought to be an autoimmune disease in which the body's immune system attacks itself. Although researchers do not understand it fully, they suspect that an unidentified virus stimulates the immune system and the disease-fighting cells inflame the joints. This disease affects the heart, lungs and eyes in addition to several joints at a time, resulting in overall stiffness and aching. It usually affects both feet or both hands at once and may produce small lumps—from the size of a pea to the size of a walnut—under the skin near the elbow, the ears or nose, the back of the scalp, over the knee or under the toes. The lumps are usually painless and present no physical problems.

Rheumatoid arthritis attacks the membrane that lines the joints, causing it to become inflamed. The cartilage, ligaments, muscles, bones and surrounding tissues deteriorate, and the joints get loose. There are blood tests that determine the presence of rheumatoid arthritis, and as the disease progresses it can be detected on X-rays. It is the most debilitating form of arthritis.

Signs and symptoms of rheumatoid arthritis include pain and swelling in the smaller joints of the hands and feet, overall aching or stiffness (especially after sleeping or sitting still for long periods). Joints are swollen, painful and warm to the touch during the first attack and following flare-ups. There may be sweats and fevers accompanied by loss of strength in the muscles surrounding the joints. Individuals with severe forms of rheumatoid arthritis usually retain flexibility in the joints and have less pain than it appears they should have. Rheumatoid arthritis is a chronic disorder, with alternate periods of remission when there is no pain, swelling, sleeplessness etc. Then there are flare ups with variable extents of severity. Rheumatoid arthritis can strike at any time but most often develops between the ages of 20 and 50.

Treatment involves a proper balance between rest and exercise, possibly using a splint at night, avoiding undue fatigue and following general principles of good nutrition. It is important to avoid obesity and take medications such as anti-inflammatory drugs, corticosteroids and other options. The physician may recommend surgical joint replacement for severely damaged joints. [5]

---

[5] Ibid.

Arthritis Intervention & Prevention

STEPS TO PREVENT OR DELAY THE ONSET OF OSTEOARTHRITIS:

Serious joint injury can lead to osteoarthritis, but usually the disease results from a combination of factors including inheritance, accounting for about half of hand and hip osteoarthritis. The following steps can prevent or delay the onset of osteoarthritis:

- Weight loss. People who lose as little as 11 pounds reduce their osteoarthritis risk by half.
- Strengthening quadriceps muscles at the front of the thigh even moderately can lead to a 20 – 30 percent decrease in the risk of osteoarthritis.
- Sports that involve high-intensity, acute, direct joint impact and those that involve repetitive twisting and impact increase the risk of osteoarthritis.
- Intake of Vitamins C and D reduces pain and protects against new and progressive osteoarthritis.
- Recognize that most osteoarthritis in males is the result of occupational activities that require squatting, kneeling and heavy lifting.

PREVENTING PROGRESSION AND DISABILITY

- Exercise strengthens muscles and improves range of motion. It also prevents joint stiffness.
- Shock-absorbing footwear helps decrease the impact of running and walking on the knees.
- Follow the instructions of your physician in all areas, in addition to an exercise program—medications, nutrition, behavior interventions and surgical treatments.[6]

---

[6] www.drkoop.com/dyncon/article.asp?at=&id=9296

CHAPTER SUMMARY

THE SKELETAL SYSTEM AND THE LEADERSHIP IN THE CHURCH ARE SIMILAR IN THAT:

- People who hold positions of leadership in the church form the framework of the church as the skeletal system forms the framework of the body.

- The integrity of leaders in the church determines the effectiveness of the church in the community as the integrity of the skeletal system determines the ability of one's physical body to stand and move about.

- Bones store minerals and when needed by the cells, minerals are available via bones. Church leaders are endowed with wisdom through the knowledge of God. When needed by members, wisdom is available from leaders.

- Bones are arranged in the body to protect and enhance the function of underlying organs. Leaders are placed in the church to protect the gospel of Christ and enhance Christ's message to individuals.

- Persons in leadership positions must know the purpose and mission for their group, the vision of the leaders at higher levels and what is expected of them.

- Bones are held together at the joints by flexible, connective tissue. Love is the connective tissue that holds the Body of Christ together.

ARTHRITIS

- Osteoarthritis usually involves only one joint such as a knee, hip, the neck or back. It is also known as wear-and-tear arthritis, a degenerative joint disease.

- Osteoarthritis is usually accompanied by bony nodules on the fingers and bony spurs on the bones of the joint involved. It is more likely to occur in elderly rather than in young people.

- Rheumatoid arthritis usually affects the joints of both hands or of both feet at the same time, causing deterioration of the structures and tissues surrounding the joint. It is a disease of the immune system attacking itself.

- Rheumatoid arthritis is the most debilitating form or arthritis and develops between ages 20 to 50.

CHAPTER SIX
The Muscular System

Muscles allow the body to move by pulling on tendons, which in turn pull on the bones to which they are connected. The fleshy portion of the muscle between the tendons is called the belly of the muscle. A very familiar muscle organ is the biceps, located in the upper arm.

- Muscle movement is based on two forces--resistance and effort. The resistance may be regarded as something to be overcome or balanced, and effort is exerted to overcome the resistance. Resistance may be the weight of the body to be moved, such as an arm or leg, or some object to be lifted, or both. The muscular effort (contraction) is applied to the bone at its insertion and brings about the work of motion or movement.

- Most body movements require the coordinated activity of several skeletal muscles. In fact, skeletal muscles usually act in groups rather than individually. As an example, think about flexing the forearm at the elbow. A muscle that causes a desired action is referred to as the agonist or prime mover. In this instance, the biceps is the agonist. At the same time that the biceps contracts (shortens), the muscle in the back of the arm—triceps, relaxes (lengthens) giving way to the movement of the biceps. If we consider the extension of the forearm at the elbow, the triceps would contract and the biceps would relax. Other muscles that assist in the movement of the arm are the deltoid and pectoralis major, synergists in that they assist in the movement.

- Skeletal muscles are connected to bones.

- Skeletal muscles consist of thousands of microscopic, long cylindrical cells lying parallel to each other. They are wrapped in a fibrous covering and are well supplied with nerves and blood vessels.

- Muscles receive messages—impulses from the nervous system—telling them where, when and how to move.

- Skeletal muscles require a large amount of nutrients and oxygen to contract and expand.

- A muscle without a functional nerve connection cannot operate.

- The production of heat by skeletal muscles is an important homeostatic mechanism for maintaining normal body temperature. Of the total energy released during muscular contraction, only 20-30 percent is used for mechanical work (contraction).

The remainder is released as heat, which is used by the body to help maintain a normal body temperature.[1]

THE MUSCULAR SYSTEM

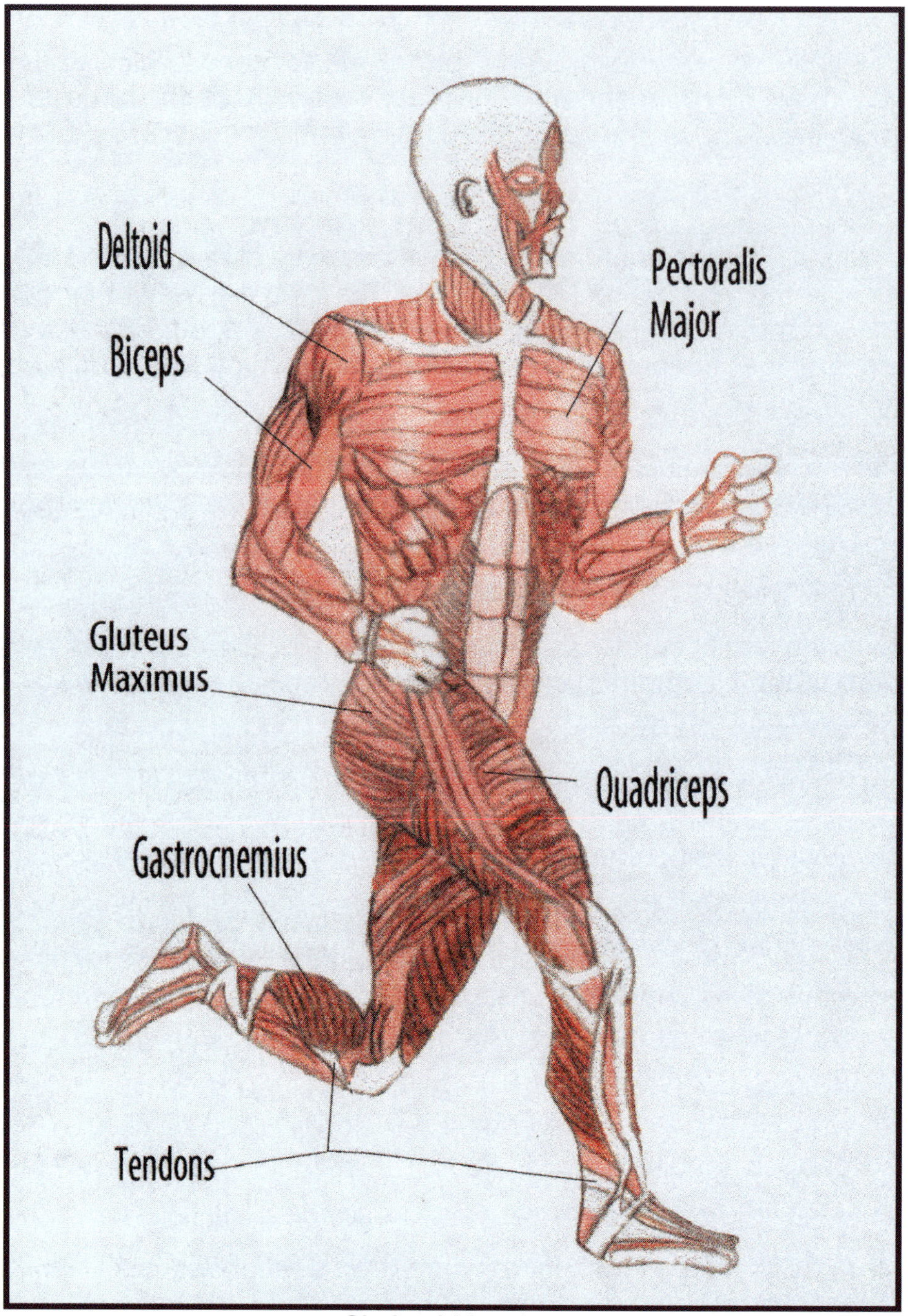

Skeletal Muscles

[1] Gerard J. Tortora and Nicholas Anagnostakos, Principles of Anatomy and Physiology (San Francisco: Canfield Press, 1975), pp. 175-187

THE MUSCULAR SYSTEM: **The Ministry Of The Church**

The various ministries in the church carry out the function of the church. They form the "musculature" of the Body of Christ. Muscles imply movement or mobility. Christ took his ministry from place to place to people who were in the routine of their daily lives. "And Jesus went about all the cities and villages, teaching in their synagogues, and preaching the gospel of the kingdom, and healing every sickness and every disease among the people." (Matthew 9:35) Jesus selected his disciples from busy people, accustomed to being in motion. One day He saw two brothers fishing, and he said to them, "Follow me, and I will make you fishers of men." (Matthew 4:19b), and they became his disciples.

The New Testament Church members were comfortable and happy while staying to themselves going house to house, sharing and breaking bread. (Acts 2:42) Potential believers found them, worshipped with them and joined them. Then, when problems of persecution arose, the church members broke away from the tightly knit family style of worship and brotherhood. They scattered about the city and the country, taking their spiritual beliefs with them, ministering to professions and nationalities that otherwise would not have been exposed to the teachings of Jesus. (Acts 8:1)

Ministries involve people in the congregation providing a service while carrying the word inside and/or outside the walls of the church. Just before he ascended to Heaven, Jesus instructed his disciples to stay in Jerusalem for a special anointing that would enable them to carry out the ministry he had begun on the earth. "But ye shall receive power, after that the Holy Ghost is come upon you: and ye shall be witnesses unto me both in Jerusalem, and in all Judaea, and in Samaria, and unto the uttermost part of the earth. " (Acts 1:8) The church flexes its muscles by carrying out Christ's ministry inside the walls of the church (Jerusalem) as well as outside within the community (Judaea) and extending to foreign missions (The uttermost parts of the earth).

While in the synagogue in Nazareth on the Sabbath day, Jesus read from the book of Isaiah about his mission on earth. "The Spirit of the Lord is upon me, because he hath anointed me to preach the gospel to the poor; he hath sent me to heal the broken hearted, to preach deliverance to the captives, and recovering of sight to the blind, to set at liberty them that are bruised, To preach the acceptable year of the Lord." (Luke 4:18,19) Jesus had a purpose to fulfill, and timing was important for him, as well as for those to whom he ministered. "He that believeth on me, the works that I do shall he do also; and greater works than these shall he do; because I go unto my Father." (John 14:12) Jesus wanted his disciples to know that they would be expected to surpass his works because of the presence of the Holy Ghost and the fact that there were more of them. He told them to, "Go ye into all the world, and preach the gospel to every creature. He that believeth and is baptized shall be saved. But he that believeth not shall be damned." (Mark 16:15,16)

The ministry of the church, therefore, is to unite (reconcile) people with God, through Christ. "And all things are of God, who hath reconciled us to himself by Jesus Christ, and hath given to us the ministry of reconciliation" (II Corinthians 5:18) After the above commission to the disciples, they and all who believed began to carry out the ministry in the most effective manner they knew. The apostle Paul said, "For though I be free from all men, yet have I made myself servant to all, that I might gain the more… I am made all things to all men, that I might by all means save some." (I Corinthians 9: 19b, 22b).

Muscle movement is based on two forces, resistance and effort. **Resistance** is the force of an object to be overcome or balanced. The weight of a box on the floor poses resistance when you want to lift it. Spiritually, resistance is the force of evil that stands against the principles of the church and must be overcome. **Effort** is the energy exerted by muscles to leverage the bones of the body to overcome the resistance and lift the box from the floor. Spiritually, effort is the power of God leveraged upon impossible situations and circumstances in the world, to bring about mental, physical and spiritual healing and to set the captives free. This is movement and motion, the function of the Body of Christ. "For we wrestle not against flesh and blood, but against principalities, against powers, against the rulers of the darkness of this world, against spiritual wickedness in high places." (Ephesians 6:12) Believers must intercept, intercede and intervene (whatever it takes) to overcome the works of evil, to win souls for Christ.

To intercept means to stop, deflect or interrupt the progress or intended course of.[2] "He which converteth the sinner from the error of his way shall save a soul from death and shall hide a multitude of sins." (James 5:20) What a blessed undertaking, to interrupt one's journey to destruction.

To intercede means to plead on another's behalf.[3] The children of Israel were at a point in the Old Testament very far from God just as the world is today. They were wicked to every extent of the imagination. Even the prophets were doing evil. The Lord said, "And I sought for a man among them, that should make up the hedge, and stand in the gap before me for the land, that I should not destroy it." (Ezekiel 22:30) Even today, the Lord is looking for believers who are willing to stand in the gap—intercede on behalf of a sinful world—to allow sinners more time to accept Him and not bring His righteous judgment upon them too soon.

To intervene means to come in or between so as to hinder or alter an action.[4] "And, having stoned Paul, drew him out of the city, supposing he had been dead. Howbeit, as the disciples stood round about him, he rose up, and came into the city: and the next day he departed with Barnabas to Derbe. " (Acts 14:19b-20) Here is a situation in which the apostle Paul was stoned and thrown out of the city by people who wanted to stop him from preaching the gospel. They thought he was dead. The disciples stood around Paul, serving as instruments used by the powerful Holy Spirit to heal his body, relieve the pain, encourage him and protect him from further injury. Paul was healed and renewed to the extent that he could leave town the next day to preach in other cities. What a powerful example of a *group intervention!*

Most bodily movements are coordinated by the activity of several skeletal muscles. Ministries in the church must be coordinated: Pastors lead and set the spiritual pace for the church; evangelists motivate; teachers explain; missionaries fulfill physical needs; choirs set the tone for worship and praise; ushers make people feel welcome and comfortable in the house of God and so on. These ministries mobilize Jesus' message

---

[2] *American Heritage College Dictionary* Third Edition (Boston, New York: Houghton Mifflin Co., 1997)
[3] Ibid.
[4] Ibid.

while caring for the spiritual and physical needs of people. They are successful when the cause of Christ is the central theme of the church. "For we are labourers together with God;" (I Corinthians 3:9a)

In a parable, Jesus told his disciples that although invitations may be given to certain people to visit and/or join congregations, they may not come. "Therefore, Go out quickly into the streets and lanes of the city, and bring in hither the poor, and the maimed, and the halt, and the blind . . . Go out into the highways and hedges and compel them to come in, that my house may be filled." (Luke14:22b, 23b) The word "go" implies movement outside comfortable boundaries. The verse also implies that we are to make it happen. Often, churches are content not to grow, quoting that "God will add to the church such as should be saved." (Acts 2:47) The operative word in this verse is "daily." *Daily* the Lord added to the church such as should be saved. We should expect regular growth to take place in the church even today. Various methods must be used to bring people to Christ. When one method or targeted group does not respond sufficiently, we must try another and so on. The Lord will bless the effort.

Skeletal muscle expands and contracts and is connected to bones. The ministry of the church requires that believers stay flexible as muscles do and be able to serve in whatever capacity is needed. This requires a humble spirit such as Jesus showed his disciples, "If I then, your Lord and Master, have washed your feet; ye also ought to wash one another's feet. For I have given you an example, that ye should do as I have done to you." (John 13:14,15) John the Baptist, the forerunner of Christ, heard from some of his followers that Jesus was baptizing, and all men came to him. John knew that his agenda was to introduce Jesus and the concept of baptism, and Jesus would take over from there as the Savior of the world. John the Baptist told them, "He must increase, but I must decrease." (John 3:30) Flexibility helps believers recognize and give preference to others when they know that God is working through them to provide the solution for the current situation.

Skeletal muscle consists of thousands of microscopic, long cylindrical cells lying parallel to each other, well supplied with nerves and blood vessels. The design of skeletal muscles, long cylindrical cells lying parallel to each other, is their source of strength. "...And be strong, all ye people of the land, saith the Lord, and work: for I am with you, saith the Lord of hosts." (Haggai 2:4b) "Finally, my brethren, be strong in the Lord, and in the power of his might." (Ephesians 6:10) The Word attributes strength to people working together and through the power of the Holy Spirit. "But ye shall receive power, after that the Holy Ghost is come upon you: and ye shall be witnesses unto me both in Jerusalem, and in all Judaea, and in Samaria, and unto the uttermost part of the earth." (Acts 1:8)

Muscles receive messages, impulses from the nervous system, on where, when and how to move. Direction for where, when and how the church is to move comes via the Holy Spirit, from Christ, who is the head of the church. (Chapter Nine) Believers are vessels through which Christ carries out his will. They are to deliver the message where, when and how it is received from God. "As every man hath received the gift, even so minister the same one to another, as good stewards of the manifold grace of God." (I Peter 4:10)

Examples of divine guidance directing believers to fill the spiritual needs of others are found in the book of Acts. Philip was sent by an angel from the villages of the Samaritans to the desert, where he was able to explain a passage of scripture and lead the Ethiopian to Christ; then he baptized him (Acts 8:26-38). Peter was directed while praying and in a trance to carry the Gospel to the Gentiles. He followed through, and they were filled with the spirit. (Acts 11:5-18) In a vision, Ananias was told to go pray with Saul, one who had been persecuting the believers. Saul had been blinded while on the road to Damascus and had miraculously become a believer. Through Ananias' prayer, Paul received his sight and began to preach the same gospel for which he had been persecuting the saints. (Acts 9:10-20)

Skeletal muscles require a large amount of nutrients and oxygen to contract and expand. In the Spiritual church, nutrients represent the Word, and oxygen represents the refreshing we experience through belief, prayer and meditation. There will be more about this in chapter eleven, the Respiratory System. Paul told the saints at the church in Colosse to "Let the word of Christ dwell in you richly in all wisdom; teaching and admonishing one another in psalms and hymns and spiritual songs, singing with grace in your hearts to the Lord." (Colossians 3:16) Having an abundance of the Word of God within supplies one with wisdom and knowledge to teach and encourage others. "And pray in the spirit on all occasions with all kinds of prayers and requests. With this in mind, be alert and always keep on praying for all the saints." (Ephesians 6:18 NIV) Believers have compassion for and are concerned about one another as Jesus was. "And Jesus went forth, and saw a great multitude, and was moved with compassion toward them, and he healed their sick." (Matthew 14:14)

A muscle without a functional nerve connection cannot operate. Muscles connected to bones without a connection to the nervous system are non-functional. Similarly, a church that is well organized and structured with various auxiliaries and organizations must be connected to the spirit of God to function as the Body of Christ. Jesus told his disciples, "It is the spirit that quickeneth; the flesh profiteth nothing: the words that I speak unto you, they are spirit, and they are life." (John 6:63) God's spirit gives life, vitality and purpose to the church organization. Through it the church gains knowledge. "Now we have received, not the spirit of the world, but the spirit which is of God; that we might know the things that are freely given to us of God." (I Corinthians 2:12) "That ye stand fast in the spirit, with one mind striving together for the faith of the gospel." (Philippians 1:27b) Paul wanted the believers to know that having the spirit of God resulted in their having knowledge of the deep things of God and that they must hold firmly to the Spirit of God and work toward a common belief in the gospel.

Of the total energy released when muscles contract, only 20-30 percent is used for moving the muscle. The remainder is released as heat, which is used by the body to help maintain a normal body temperature. God requires a lot of believers. For starters, they have to give up personal rewards and vendettas, give time and money to the church and to people in need, then avoid functions that satisfy the flesh. As Paul so succinctly said, "I beseech you therefore, brethren, by the mercies of God, that ye present your bodies a living sacrifice, holy, acceptable unto God, which is your reasonable service." (Romans 12:1)

Consider, however, running in a benefit marathon on a cool day to generate financial assistance for an organization that assists battered women. As you run, the muscles of your legs and arms keep stretching and contracting rapidly; you take deeper breaths in and out. At the end of the race, your accomplishments are many: Externally and most evident, monies have been raised for the "cause." Internally, your body has generated heat and kept itself warm in the cool air. Your heart has pumped at a faster rate and established more efficient circulation for itself and the rest of your body. Your lungs have expanded and provided surplus oxygen for the cells of your body. You have initiated a process by which your blood pressure and cholesterol levels can be reduced, and your bones have added density (solid). The personal benefits of this exercise are many, even while supporting the cause.

In a similar way, Jesus said, "But seek ye first the kingdom of God, and his righteousness; and all these things shall be added unto you." (Matthew 6:33) In the Old Testament, Moses described God's blessings that benefit us personally when we are obedient in service to him, "And ye shall serve the Lord your God, and he shall bless thy bread, and thy water; and I will take sickness away from the midst of thee. There shall nothing cast their young, nor be barren, in thy land: the number of thy days I will fulfil. I will send my fear before thee, and will destroy all the people to whom thou shalt come, and I will make all thine enemies turn their backs unto thee." (Exodus 23:25-27)

Some of the **personal rewards** of serving the Lord include his blessings on your food and water, greater health and wellness, greater potential to bear children, a full life span, divine assistance in fighting your battles and in conquering your enemies, and evidence of God's strength will bring fear into the enemy camp, causing them to leave you alone.

There are many **spiritual rewards** of serving within the Body of Christ. The church will prosper, members will enjoy greater health and wellness, there will be no spiritual miscarriages resulting in lost souls among you, people within the congregation will have a greater opportunity to be reborn and grow to spiritual maturity, and the body of Christ will have greater potential to grow in size and effectiveness. Enemies of Christ, confronted by people empowered by the grace of the Holy Spirit and the armor of God, will turn and run, due to the fear of God. The results of believers flexing the spiritual muscles of the Body of Christ, causing it to walk, talk and move about the earth, should be felt throughout the community.

God's rewards are not limited to things on this earth. "Then shall the King say unto them on his right hand, Come, ye blessed of my Father, inherit the kingdom prepared for you from the foundation of the world: For I was an hungred, and ye gave me meat; I was thirsty, and ye gave me drink: I was a stranger, and ye took me in: Naked, and ye clothed me: I was sick, and ye visited me: I was in prison, and ye came unto me." (Matthew 25:34-36)

THE MUSCULAR SYSTEM ■ PATHOLOGY

Strains and Sprains

MUSCLE STRAIN

Muscle strains are also known as "pulled muscles," which occur when you place too great a demand on a muscle. Minor strains are caused when we overstretch or overwork an area of the body, causing the muscle to be sore, but it does not lose its strength.

Serious muscle strains occur when the muscle is exerted to the extent that it causes some of the fibers to tear and bleed internally. In rare instances, a muscle is ruptured when all of the fibers are torn apart entirely.

The hamstrings are the most common muscles to strain. It is a group of muscles located at the back of the thigh and enables you to bend your knee and extend your thigh, the motions that are required for running. Another common muscle injury is known as the groin pull (strain). It may result from repetitive overuse or a single traumatic event and involves muscles of the groin, including the abdomen, leg and pelvic areas.

Signs and symptoms of a muscle strain include pain in a specific area, followed by tenderness and, sometimes, swelling. During the 24 hours after the incident, stiffness can be expected. If the muscle has no function at all, it could be ruptured.

SPRAINS

A true sprain involves damage to the ligaments—tough bands of stretchy tissue that connect the ends of bones forming a joint. Sprains are a result of a violent twist or stretch of the joint, forcing it outside its normal range of movement. The ligaments are left stretched or torn. Usually, sprains occur in joints of the ankles, knees and arches of the foot when a fall or stumble causes the weight of your body to be placed on the joint in an unnatural position.

Signs and symptoms of a sprain include rapid swelling, impaired joint function, pain and tenderness in the area and, possibly, discoloration of the skin. The degree of sprains may be mild, moderate or severe, depending on the extent of the damage to the ligament, whether stretched, slightly torn, or completely torn. Emergency care is necessary if you hear a popping sound and you are immediately unable to move the joint or if the pain and difficulty moving the joint lasts for more than two or three days. In most cases, you will be able to bear weight on a sprained joint within 24 hours, and it will be fully healed within two weeks.

TREATMENT

After spraining a ligament or straining a muscle, it is best to use cold treatment for one to three days, to reduce swelling and inflammation. Swelling decreases the amount of blood flow to the area and the amount of oxygen available to the cells, causing damage to tissues. Cold applications slow the metabolism of cells and allow tissues to survive the temporary lack of oxygen. It also controls bleeding into the tissues and reduces pain.
Heat should be used only after swelling and bleeding have stopped. It reduces pain and prepares muscles for strengthening exercises during rehabilitation.[5]

[5] David E. Larson, M.D. Mayo Clinic Family Health Book, Second Edition, (New York: William Morrow and Company Inc., 1996), pp. 868-869

THE MUSCULAR SYSTEM ♥ HEALTH & WELLNESS
Benefits of Physical Exercise

To begin to exercise, for those who have not done so, requires a change in mindset, planning and a commitment to a higher level of health and wellness. Commitment means that the behavior will continue whether or not it is enjoyed. The form of exercise should fit into your life-style. Sometimes it helps to sustain interest when you vary the exercise routine from day to day. Often we admire the physically fit appearance of others and think it is natural for them, but they are actually practicing some form of exercise. We can accomplish the same outcomes with a plan and discipline. So, let your mind control your body and get started on some form of daily exercise. The benefits are unlimited. Regular exercise:

- Reduces **blood pressure** – By causing relaxation of the mind and arteries.
- Reduces the **heart rate** – By increasing the efficiency of each contraction of the heart muscle, the heart does not have to contract as rapidly.
- Reduces **blood cholesterol** – Burns fat.
- Reduces **stress** – Relaxes the mind, puts you in control, stimulates a positive attitude.
- Improves **circulation** in the veins and arteries – Veins and arteries relax, allowing blood to flow through them freely.
- Promotes **collateral circulation** in the heart – Veins and arteries of the heart form additional routes for getting blood to the cells of the heart.
- Increases **lung capacity** – Causes you to breath deeper.
- Decreases **respiratory rate** at rest – Increased efficiency of the lungs.
- Releases **endorphins** - You feel in control; your attitude improves.
- Strengthens **bones** – Stimulates bone cells to reproduce.
- Causes **weight** loss – Burns calories.
- Strengthens **muscles** - Improves muscle tone.

CHAPTER SUMMARY

The Muscular System And The Ministry Of The Church:

- Skeletal muscles exert themselves against the forces of resistance utilizing efforts of will. The ministry of the church exerts itself against the forces of evil utilizing divine inspiration, power and the grace of God.

- Movement of an arm or leg requires coordination of the actions of several muscles. Ministries in the church must be coordinated so that they do not contradict or interfere with each other.

- Muscles expand and contract because of their flexibility. Flexibility in believers causes them to honor and prefer one another in place of themselves, when the Holy Spirit is working.

- The long, cylindrical skeletal muscle cells lying parallel to each other is their source of strength. The apostle Paul taught believers that their strength is in working together and comes from the Holy Spirit.

- The direction for physical muscles comes from the nervous system, as the spiritual direction (where, when and how) of the church comes via the Holy Spirit.

- Skeletal muscles require a large amount of nutrients and oxygen to contract and expand. The ministry of the church requires much prayer and study of the Word to operate effectively.

- A church ministry without a direct connection to Christ through the Holy Spirit becomes paralyzed, as does a person's muscles when severed from the nervous system.

- Muscles, releasing energy when they move, benefit the body, since their effort produces and retains usable body heat. Believers working for the cause of Christ accomplish the task at hand and simultaneously receive personal physical and spiritual blessings from God.

The Benefits Of Physical Exercise:

- To start an exercise routine requires a change in mindset, planning, commitment and behavior change.

- The benefits of physical exercise are unlimited.

CHAPTER SEVEN
The Reproductive System

The function of the female reproductive system is to produce mature eggs. Once fertilized, the embryo (fertilized egg) embeds itself into the lining of the uterus, where it is protected and nourished until it is ready for birth. This chapter will focus on the uterus as the female reproductive organ, spermatozoan, which is the male sperm, and genetic inheritance.

THE ROLE OF THE MALE

- The male reproductive system produces sperm and delivers them to the female reproductive tract.
- Even though only a single spermatozoan fertilizes an egg, it is believed that fertilization requires the combined action of a tremendous number of spermatozoa.

THE FEMALE ORGAN CENTRAL TO REPRODUCTION IS THE UTERUS

- The uterus is a hollow, pear shaped organ.
- The entire uterus is connected to the nervous system by many nerves.
- The functions of the uterus are to:
    1. Anchor and protect a fertilized egg—ovum.
    2. Provide an optimal environment while the fetus develops.
    3. Push the fetus out at birth.
    4. Exchange fetal and maternal substances through the placenta.[1]

GENETIC INHERITANCE:

- The passage of hereditary traits from one generation to another.
- Dominant genes control a particular trait; expressions of recessive genes are suppressed by the dominant gene.[2]

GROWTH AND DEVELOPMENT:

Infancy, toddler, childhood, adolescence, young adult, adulthood.

---

[1] Kathryn L McCance and Sue E. Huether Pathophysiology: The Biologic Basis for Disease in Adults and Children Third Edition (St. Louis: Mosby 1998), pp. 709-713

[2] Gerard J. Tortora and Nicholas Anagnostakos, Principles of Anatomy and Physiology (San Francisco: Canfield Press, 1975), pp. 576-582

THE REPRODUCTIVE SYSTEM

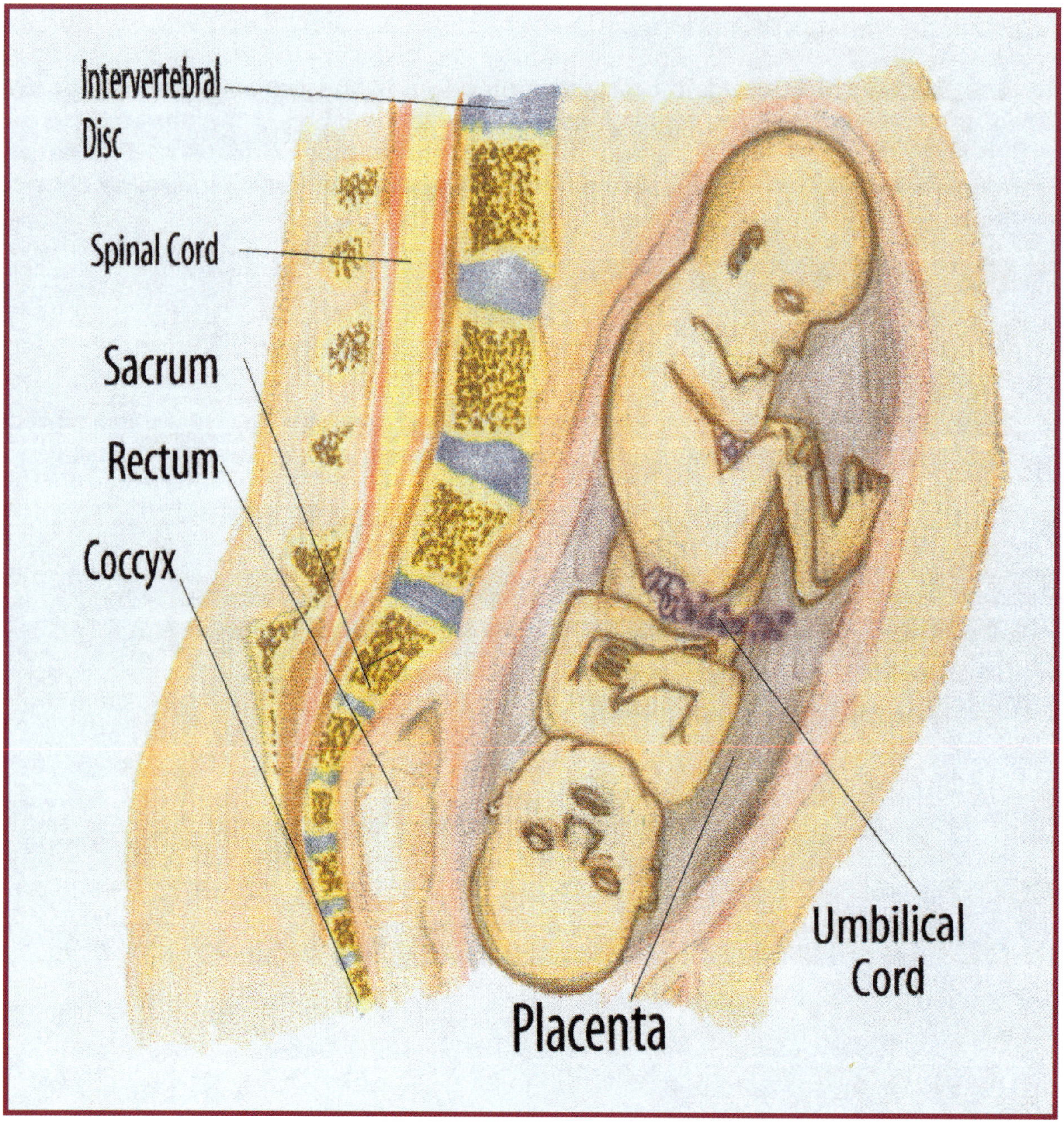

An impregnated Uterus/Womb

THE REPRODUCTIVE SYSTEM

The Church – The Womb of the Body of Christ

"And the Lord God formed man of the dust of the ground, and breathed into his nostrils the breath of life; and man became a living soul." (Genesis 2:7) God's divine breath going into Adam and Eve gave them a divine nature, a touch of deity. The three of them enjoyed a special friendship and spiritual relationship in the beautiful Garden of Eden. Adam and Eve loved and worshipped God.

One day Adam and Eve disobeyed God. Their spiritual relationship with God and the innocence between them was destroyed. As a result God removed them physically out of the Garden and took from them his divine breath of life—his spirit—and consequently their divine nature. This state of separation from God became known as spiritually dead, or in "sin." From that point on, all of mankind, including Adam and Eve's children, have been born in sin, spiritually dead. "Wherefore, as by one man sin entered into the world, and death by sin; and so death passed upon all men, for that all have sinned." (Romans 5:12) The Psalmist said, "Surely I was sinful at birth, sinful from the time my mother conceived me." (Psalm 51:5 NIV)

Within the human intellect lies an innate longing to look to, reach for and worship the Almighty God. The Psalmist again said, "From the end of the earth will I cry unto thee, when my heart is overwhelmed: lead me to the rock that is higher than I." (Psalm 61:2) God, on the other hand, who made man in his own image, has a desire for man to *recover* from his state of sin and *reconcile* with Him so that He can *restore* man's divine nature and their spiritual relationship to its original state. Job said, "But it is the spirit in a man, the breath of the Almighty, that gives him understanding." (Job 32:8 NIV)

God initiated the practice of man sacrificing a clean animal periodically to show remorse for his sins and to reconcile their relationship. However, this was a temporary fix, since man was continuously sinful. As time passed in the Old Testament, God's chosen people, the Israelites, became increasingly evil, and the sacrifices became distasteful and insufficient to God. "To what purpose is the multitude of your sacrifices unto me? saith the Lord: I am full of the burnt offerings of rams, and the fat of fed beasts; and I delight not in the blood of bullocks, or of lambs, or of he goats." (Isaiah 1:11) In his anger with Israel at another time, God said, "For I desired mercy, and not sacrifice; and the knowledge of God more than burnt offerings." (Hosea 6:6) Rather than practice forgiveness and mercy, the people took out their frustrations and revenge on one another, then covered it with a sacrifice for forgiveness. This was unacceptable to God not only because they were not getting to know Him but because continuing a life of sin ultimately meant physical death for his people. "For the wages of sin is death." (Romans 6:23a)

God set in motion a plan of salvation to offer the Israelites a plan whereby animals would no longer be sacrificed for sins and priests would no longer make repeated sacrifices that did not clear the conscience of man. These carnal ordinances (rituals of man) were entirely eliminated when Jesus, the Son of God, became the supreme sacrifice for our sin, shed his blood and died. He conquered death and hell, arose again and ascended to heaven to sit at the right hand of the Father and became our high priest. (Hebrews 9:9-11 paraphrased) "For Christ did not enter a man-made sanctuary that was only a copy of the true one; he entered heaven itself, now to appear for us in God's presence. Nor did he enter heaven to offer himself again and again, the way the high priest enters the Most Holy Place every year with blood that is not his own… But now he has appeared once for all at the end of the ages to do away with sin by the sacrifice of himself. Just as man is destined to die once, and after that to face judgment, so Christ was sacrificed once to take away the sins of many people;" (Hebrews 9:24-28a NIV)

God's revelation of a masterful plan, the coming of Christ his son, evolved over many years through prophecies in the Old Testament. Once fulfilled, God's plan provided the opportunity for mankind to re-establish a personal relationship with God as Adam and Eve had enjoyed in the Garden of Eden. "For as by one man's disobedience many were made sinners, so by the obedience of one shall many be made righteous," (Romans 5:19) "For God so loved the world that he gave his only begotten son, that whosoever believeth in him should not perish but have everlasting life." (John 3:16) Believers celebrate and refer to themselves as "saved," meaning they have been delivered from the penalty of sin, which is death, because Jesus' blood paid the penalty for all, and God has restored their divine nature and spiritual state. God created man to seek him and offers the opportunity for salvation to everyone. Believers must feed and protect the spirit and souls of those near them until they are ready for the spiritual birth, as the uterus protects the embryo and fetus until it is ready for physical birth.

The Bible identifies the church as the bride of Christ. "And I John saw the holy city, New Jerusalem, coming down from God out of heaven, prepared as a bride adorned for her husband." (Revelations 21:2). "Let us be glad and rejoice, and give honour to him: for the marriage of the Lamb is come, and his wife hath made herself ready." (Revelations 19:7). The biblical depiction of the church in the female gender leads to parallels of the church with the organs of the female reproductive system.

The function of the church is to produce mature believers by protecting and nurturing them from their first state of awareness of Jesus to a point when they accept him as personal savior and progress to the level of transcendence, when they nurture and bring others to him. There is a spiritual *quickening* as well as a legal process of adoption, which results in the birth of sons and daughters of God. "But because of His great love for us, God, who is rich in mercy, made us alive with Christ, even when we were dead in transgressions." (Ephesians 2:4-5aNIV) "But when the fulness of the time was come, God sent forth his Son, made of a woman, made under the law, To redeem them that were under the law, that we might receive the adoption of sons. And because ye are sons, God hath sent forth the Spirit of his Son into your hearts, crying, Abba, Father. Wherefore thou art no more a servant, but a son; and if a son, then an heir of God through Christ." (Galatians 4:4-7)

The male reproductive system produces sperm and delivers them to the female reproductive tract. The prophet Jeremiah wrote, "The Lord hath appeared of old unto me, saying, Yea, I have loved thee with an everlasting love: therefore with lovingkindness have I drawn thee." (Jeremiah 31:3) At some point in everyone's life, their spirit and soul (heart and mind) feel the pull of the Lord. How they respond depends partially on the degree and quality of the spiritual nurturing and guidance they have received from believers until that time in their lives. When the child Samuel heard the call of the Lord, he was unsure of how to respond until Eli the priest told him to answer, "Speak Lord, for thy servant heareth." (I Samuel 3:9) Isaiah wrote, "With my soul have I desired thee in the night; yea, with my spirit within me will I seek thee early:" (Isaiah 26:9) Isaiah knew that the desire he felt inside was from the Almighty God. God has created fertile souls, and the community of believers in the church must help complete the fertilization process and nurture them to a spiritual birth. When people search for the higher power and do not recognize or connect with the living God, in despair they sometimes create false gods to worship, turning to darkness and evil ways. It is important for believers to communicate and live sound spiritual and moral principles, because one never knows who is looking for guidance and could be led by example and instruction to recognize God's call upon their lives.

Fertilization requires the combined action of a tremendous number of spermatozoa. It takes the efforts of many believers to cultivate the Word in a person's mind to the point it takes root, is fertilized or comes to life. Paul said of his ministry, "I have planted, Apollos watered; but God gave the increase." (I Corinthians 3:6). The apostle Peter wrote to the believers, "Now that you have purified yourselves by obeying the truth so that you have sincere love for your brothers, love one another deeply, from the heart. For you have been born again, not of perishable seed, but of imperishable, through the living and enduring word of God." (I Peter 1:22,23 NIV) All believers are born as a result of God having planted his incorruptible seed in the heart, where it stays until it is cultivated and aroused by the sincere love of believers in the Body of Christ.

The uterus is a muscular, hollow, pear shaped organ. The muscle of the uterus expands from the size of a regular light bulb to a size large enough to accommodate a baby ten pounds and more and even multiple fetuses. The Body of Christ can accommodate and nurture an unlimited number of souls. Jesus said, "Come unto me, all ye that labour and are heavy laden, and I will give you rest. Take my yoke upon you, and learn of me; for I am meek and lowly in heart: and ye shall find rest unto your souls." (Matthew 11:28, 29) Jesus did not set limits or conditions on those he invited. He committed to give them relief. In fact, he told the disciples not to forbid the children whom they found to be burdensome. "But Jesus said, suffer little children, and forbid them not, to come unto me; for of such is the kingdom of heaven." (Matthew 19:14)

The entire uterus is connected to the nervous system by many nerves. The nervous system is to the physical body what the Godhead is to the church. (see Chapter Nine). God told Ezekiel about His plan to clean up the filthiness of His people, referring to the time when they would be led by the Holy Spirit rather than the laws of the Ten Commandments. "A new heart also will I give you, and a new spirit will I put within you: and I will take away the stony heart out of your flesh, and I will give you an heart of flesh. And I will put my spirit within you, and cause you to walk in my statutes, and ye shall keep my judgments, and do them." (Ezekiel 36:26,27) The indwelling Holy Spirit—electing whom, how, where and when—directs believers to lead others to Christ.

The fertilized ovum (egg) is anchored and protected in the uterus. Jesus was a defender—protector—of the weak. He defended the sinner woman who washed his feet in her tears, dried them with her hair and anointed them with oil from an alabaster box. When the Pharisee questioned Jesus' sense of propriety, Jesus said, "Her sins, which are many, are forgiven." (Luke 7:47) When the group of men and officers from the chief priests and Pharisees came to capture Jesus, he said "Whom seek ye? And they said

Jesus of Nazareth. Jesus answered, "I have told you that I am he; if therefore ye seek *me*, let these go their way:" (John 18:7,8) He negotiated with the soldiers who came to kill him for the release of his disciples who were with him. He protected them because they were his.

The uterus provides an optimal environment while the fetus (baby in the uterus) develops. In the uterus the fetus finds warmth, room to grow and contentment. In the presence of believers, potential believers—those contemplating salvation—should find a similar environment. There should be examples to follow as mentors, room to grow, encouragement, forgiveness, acceptance, guidance, patience and emotional support as well as someone to lead them to Christ once they decide to repent. Jesus said, "All that the Father giveth me shall come to me; and him that cometh to me I will in no wise cast out." (John 6:37) Peter tells us that, "The Lord is not slack concerning his promise, as some men count slackness; but is longsuffering to us-ward, not willing that any should perish, but that all should come to repentance." (II Peter 3:9)

Fetal and maternal substances are exchanged in the uterus through the placenta. The placenta collects nutrition from the mother and waste from the fetus, exchanging them according to the needs of the fetus. Jesus made provisions for all of his followers to be spiritually nourished. He asked Peter, "Simon, son of Jonas, lovest thou me more than these? He saith unto him, Yea, Lord; Thou knowest that I love thee. He saith unto him, Feed my lambs." (John 21:15) Jesus asked the same question again, and receiving the same answer, he said, "Feed my sheep." First, Jesus tested Peter's level of commitment to the cause of Christ, because it takes dedication to feed souls. Then, having heard three times from Peter that he was committed, Jesus told him to feed his lambs and sheep, covering all levels of spiritual maturity. Jesus also provided physical food for the multitudes who listened to his teaching. (Matthew 14:15-21)

The uterus pushes the fetus out at birth. Spiritual birth occurs when a person has faith in the power of God to believe that God can effect a change in his or her life. "The word is near you; it is in your mouth and in your heart, that is, the word of faith we are proclaiming: That if you confess with your mouth, 'Jesus is Lord,' and believe in your heart that God raised him from the dead, you will be saved. For it is with your heart that you believe and are justified, and it is with your mouth that you confess and are saved." (Romans 10:8b-10NIV)

Getting one to this point is a labor of love and patience for believers, varying in terms of the amount of time and nurturing it takes. Potential believers whose answer is "yes" when first approached about beginning a relationship with Christ have already been in the process of developing faith and belief in Christ. Frequently, however, this process takes time. The Lord told Isaiah, "Shall the earth be made to bring forth in one day? Or shall a nation be born at once? For as soon as Zion travailed, she brought forth her children." (Isaiah 66:8b) Everyone will not be converted in one day, just as a nation is not born all at once. But, when believers travail, toil or work hard to present Christ in their way of life, they spiritually nurture potential believers to a higher level of faith in him. Then when they decide to believe for their own salvation, souls will be born into the Body of Christ.

"And when ye see this, your heart shall rejoice, and your bones shall flourish like an herb: and the hand of the Lord shall be known toward his servants." (Isaiah 66:14) Witnessing the birth of new believers and growth In the Body of Christ make hearts rejoice and the church strong, then it is obvious to the world that the favor of God is toward his people.

Genetic inheritance is the passage of hereditary traits from one generation to another. "For by grace are ye saved through faith; and that not of yourselves: it is the gift of God." (Ephesians 2:8) Through God, under the anointing of the Holy Spirit, souls are born into the church. "Which were born, not of blood, nor of the will of the flesh, nor of the will of man, but of God." (John 1:13) God's grace, undeserved favor, extended to man creates the *opportunity* for man to allow God to enter his life. Faith and belief on the part of man creates the *opportunity* for God to implant His spirit in man, which is also in his Son, resulting in a new, born again believer. "And because ye are sons, God hath sent forth the Spirit of his Son into your hearts, crying Abba, Father." (Galatians 4:6) "Therefore if any man be in Christ, he is a new creature: old things are passed away; behold, all things are become new." (II Corinthians 5:17)

The celebrating and rejoicing flows freely when souls are born into the Body of Christ. But this is not the end. It is really the beginning of life for the new believer. Paul told the Galatians, "My little children, of whom I travail in birth *again* until Christ be *formed* in you," (Galatians 4:19). As a newborn baby has inherited traits of its parents, so new believers inherit the Spirit of Christ. Paul prayed that the new Christians would allow Christ-like traits to develop and mature in themselves. "That the God of our Lord Jesus Christ, the Father of glory, may give unto you the spirit of wisdom and revelation in the knowledge of him; The eyes of your understanding being enlightened; that ye may know what is the hope of his calling, and what the riches of the glory of his inheritance in the saints, and what is the exceeding greatness of his power to us-ward who believe, according to the working of his mighty power." (Ephesians 1:17-19) The next step for the believer is to receive the Holy Spirit, which God gives to them that ask. (Luke 11:13)

Dominant genes control a particular trait; expression of recessive genes is suppressed by the dominant gene. After being quickened by the Spirit of God, believers must make a conscious decision to allow God's spirit to dominate their natural sinful nature, to the extent that it becomes suppressed like recessive genes. The dominant traits of the Spirit of God are described in the Bible as the Fruit of the Spirit: Love, joy, peace, longsuffering, gentleness, meekness, temperance, goodness and faith. (Galatians 5:22) The merit of these genes will be discussed in chapter ten. Additional traits of believers that come from the dominant spiritual genes include the ability to be overcomers and forgiving. "Ye are of God, little children, and have overcome them: because greater is he that is in you, than he that is in the world." (I John 4:4) "For whatsoever is born of God overcometh the world: and this is the victory that overcometh the world, even our faith." (I John 5:4) "And be ye kind one to another, tenderhearted, forgiving one another, even as God for Christ's sake hath forgiven you." (Ephesians 4:32)

The Spirit of God recognizes believers when it finds Christ's Spirit in them. "The Spirit itself beareth witness with our spirit, that we are the children of God: And if children, then heirs; heirs of God, and joint-heirs with Christ." (Romans 8:16,17a) "Nevertheless the foundation of God standeth sure, having this seal, the Lord knoweth them that are his. And, Let every one that nameth the name of Christ depart from inquity." (II Timothy 2:19)

The seed of the righteous: There is a very special population of potential believers who the writer believes require special treatment. They are children of believers who were reared in the environment of the church and now avoid all resemblance of Christianity in their lives. These are frequently children who accepted Christ as their savior at some point but lacking maturity and because of observed inconsistencies in the lives and testimonies of churchgoers, or for other reasons, have turned away from God. These people hold a special place in God's heart, and he has made a commitment to their parents. "Though hand join in hand, the wicked shall not be unpunished: but the seed of the righteous shall be delivered." (Proverbs 11:21)

Believers who have heirs in this position must request wisdom of the Lord that their actions and words nurture the seed that was planted and made fertile by God. These children need tough love in earthly matters and an abundance of love, encouragement, patience and travail for their spirits. There is a critical balance to be considered between battering them about the punitive judgments of God and feeding them God's word of love and promises. God told Jeremiah, "Yea, I have loved thee with an everlasting love: therefore with lovingkindness have I drawn thee." (Jeremiah 31:3) To allow patience to grow thin and continuously batter these souls with God's punishment could very well cause them to reject asking God into their life and to abort God's seed within.

Parents must tell these heirs about God's commitment to deliver them from bondage and how by faith they as parents are expecting God to fulfill that promise. They should be reminded often that their "close calls" with death, the law, or substance abuse are proof that God is watching over them. Lead them to give thanks to God for each incident, and you will notice them looking for opportunities to tell you how God has helped them. Tell them how the prayers of a parent are effective, but their own prayer for help, guidance and deliverance would be most effective. Encouragement of this kind gives them *hope.* Hope nurtures the Word deep inside and fortifies their tiny seed of faith in God. Believers should reach out to other believers' children by giving them a word of encouragement and assistance along with scriptural guidance, believing that as they do for the children of other believers, so shall it be done to their children. "Cast thy bread upon the waters: for thou shalt find it after many days." (Ecclesiastes 11:1)

God told Jeremiah about the voice of his people crying out to Him, "Is not the Lord in Zion? ... The harvest is past, the summer is ended, and we are not saved." (Jeremiah 8:19b,20) These people were heirs of Abraham, Joseph, Manasseh and Gilead and had been taught God's ways. They knew that they were on the wrong track, a long way from where they should be. They also knew to call out to God for help. God asked the Prophet Jeremiah, "Is there no balm in Gilead; is there no physician there? why then is not the health of the daughter of my people recovered?" (Jeremiah 8:22) When we know the Word and right from wrong, God holds us responsible for others. The songwriter wrote a response: There is *"A Balm In Gilead"* to save the sin sick soul.[3]

Growth and development take place over an extended period of time, and expectations increase with each stage. "Now I say, that the heir, as long as he is a child, differeth nothing from a servant, though he be lord of all; But is under tutors and

[3] Author unknown ; African-American Spiritual

governors until the time appointed of the father." (Galatians 4:1-2) Though newly born believers are sons and daughters of God and heirs of the promise, they are still in need of training and support from the Body of Christ. It is important at all stages of spiritual, emotional and physical growth to receive the necessary elements for optimal health and wellness. "Train up a child in the way he should go: and when he is old, he will not depart from it." (Proverbs 22:6)

Persistence in prayer is essential for the well-being of all believers that they will be overcomers and not fail. Jesus told his disciple Simon Peter, "Simon, Simon, behold, Satan hath desired to have you, that he may sift you as wheat: But I have prayed for thee, that thy faith fail not: and when thou art converted, strengthen thy brethren." (Luke 22:31,32)

At a time in history when the Israelites were living wicked and evil lives, Daniel, who had been taught the ways and statutes of the Lord, spoke to God on behalf of the nation for pardon. After some time of presenting his case in prayer to God for the sins of his people, the angel Gabriel appeared to him and said, "O Daniel, I am now come forth to give thee skill and understanding.... For thou art greatly beloved..." (Daniel 9:22, 23) Daniel was given a vision and an understanding of God's plan for Israel's recovery from that time in history extending far into the future. Due to his growth and dedication to God as well as his people, Daniel was given a tremendous responsibility to write the vision that gives insight into the future even for us today. "For unto whomsoever much is given, of him shall be much required: and to whom men have committed much, of him they will ask the more" (Luke 12:48b)

God has a plan for our lives. He told Jeremiah, "Before I formed thee in the belly I knew thee; and before thou camest forth out of the womb I sanctified thee (set aside for a special purpose), and I ordained thee a prophet unto the nations." (Jeremiah 1:5)

THE REPRODUCTIVE SYSTEM ■ PATHOLOGY
Teen Pregnancy and Abortion

TEEN PREGNANCY

The United States has the highest rate of teen age pregnancy of any Western industrialized nation. More than a third of American girls become pregnant at least once during adolescence, and most of them carry their pregnancy to term. One-third of adolescent mothers get pregnant again before the end of their teen age years. Adolescent pregnancy and childbirth have reached epidemic proportions in many inner-city communities, and most of the pregnancies are unplanned and unwanted.

There are multiple, complex factors that play a part in teen pregnancies. Some of the factors are peer pressure for premarital sex, the teen's desire to be loved, low self-esteem, lack of knowledge about the physiology of conception and substance abuse. Pregnancy can occur after having sexual intercourse only once. One-half of teen age pregnancies occur within six months after teen agers become sexually active.

Teen agers are not prepared for the responsibilities of parenting, either financially or emotionally. Although it takes two to bring a baby into the world, the female usually makes the greater sacrifice in parenting the infant. School districts may or may not have special programs to help pregnant adolescents continue their education. Education, employment and friendships are at risk of being lost; yet, most pregnant teen agers keep and raise their babies. Although teen age fathers are just as responsible for the pregnancy and should participate in caring for and supporting their children, statistics show that most do not.

Girls should see a physician as soon as possible when they realize they are pregnant. Teen agers are themselves still growing and need more medical care during pregnancy than mature women do, though they usually receive less. Teen agers are also at higher risk for complications of pregnancy such as miscarriage, abnormally slow growth of the fetus, stillbirths and premature births. These complications are not so much related to age as to youthful mothers' ignorance about taking care of themselves. They may have inadequate diets and little or no prenatal care, which may result in more frequent cases of preeclampsia and eclampsia—often called toxemia—a potentially fatal condition.[4]

ABORTION

Although abortion is defined as "terminating a pregnancy," it actually involves terminating a life. Therapeutic abortions are done for medical reasons involving the mental and/or physical health of the mother, while elective abortions are a matter of convenience. Elective abortions are not considered an option for believers, so other alternatives such as abstinence and adoption should be utilized. Therapeutic abortions should be considered on a case-by-case basis and only with sincere fasting and prayer.

THE REPRODUCTIVE SYSTEM ♥ HEALTH & WELLNESS
Healthy Pregnancy, Healthy Baby

HEALTHY PREGNANCY

In the ideal world, pregnancy is planned between a husband and wife based on their financial stability, emotional stability, commitment to each other and responsibility to the child they are creating.

Before attempting to become pregnant, a woman should see her physician for a complete physical examination. She may have conditions such as high blood pressure, pelvic tumors, anemia or diabetes without manifesting symptoms. If present, such conditions would seriously complicate pregnancy and can be detected easily during a comprehensive physical exam.

If a medical condition is detected, the physician can help her get it under control before she attempts to become pregnant. If a particular disease or genetic abnormality runs in her family, an expert in genetic counseling can advise her. The physician will review with her any complications of previous pregnancies, the potential for recurrence and, if necessary, she may be referred to an obstetrician for intervention.

Assuming that she has been determined to be in good health by her physician, it is time to examine her life-style. If she is overweight and wants to reduce, it should be done before becoming pregnant. Pregnancy is not the time to begin a diet. If a cigarette smoker, she should quit smoking because during pregnancy, smoking causes a greater

---

[4] David E. Larson, M.D. Mayo Clinic Family Health Book Second Edition (New York: William Morrow and Company Inc., 1996), pp. 147-174

incidence of miscarriages and stillbirths, and babies have lower than normal birth weight, which could cause developmental problems later. If she takes prescription or over-the-counter medications, she should check with her physician about whether or not to continue taking them. She should not drink alcohol.

The first sign of pregnancy is an interruption of her menstrual cycle. Tender or painful breasts, morning sickness that may extend to later times of the day, fatigue and frequent urination are symptoms that may follow. Pregnancy should be confirmed by a pregnancy test, and then prenatal visits should begin.

A woman's first prenatal visit involves completing a detailed health history form. It will ask questions about her family medical history and overall health to determine whether there are any health conditions that may cause complications. A comprehensive physical exam will be done, including pelvic, blood and urine tests. Regular monthly visits follow with monitoring of blood pressure, weight and urine. It is a good practice for her to write down questions to ask the physician when she goes to her scheduled appointments. With a Doppler instrument the physician will allow the mother to be to hear the baby's heartbeat after 10 to 12 weeks, and an ultrasound will be done when considered necessary, as the baby completes the nine-month gestational period.

Nutrients the body needs during pregnancy are: **protein** (building blocks for the baby's cells and for a reserve for the mother's labor and delivery), **carbohydrates** (energy source for mother and baby and protein for tissue growth), **fats** (energy for long-term growth, especially critical for the baby's brain development), **fluids** (fluid for the amniotic sac prevents constipation and dry skin), **vitamin A** (supplement for healthy skin, eyesight, and bone growth), **vitamin C** (supplement for healthy gums, teeth and bones for baby and to improve iron absorption), **folic acid** (supplement for blood cells and hemoglobin formation), **calcium** (supplement for strong bones and teeth) and **iron** (supplement to the red blood cells that deliver oxygen to baby and mother and prevent fatigue).

The best food sources for the required nutrients are eggs, lean red meats, poultry, fish, cheese, milk, dried peas, beans, whole-grain and fortified breads and cereals, fruits, vegetables, rice, pasta, potatoes, nuts, seeds, peanut butter, oils, margarine, butter, tap and bottled water, soups, sweet potatoes, carrots, dark leafy greens, cantaloupe, apricots, citrus fruits, broccoli, tomatoes, peppers, berries, melons, potatoes with skin, bananas, yogurt, collard greens, kale, sardines and canned salmon (with bones), spinach, tofu, dried fruits.[5]

HEALTHY BABY

At the moment of birth a newborn undergoes profound physiological changes. He/she is released from a warm, snug, darkened, liquid-filled environment in which all basic needs were met to a chilly, glaring, unbounded gravity-based outside world. Within minutes the newborn must start breathing and the circulatory system must accommodate oxygen from the air. Within 24 hours, the nervous system, kidneys, endocrine, digestive and metabolic functions must operate competently in order for the newborn to live.

---

[5] David E. Larson, M.D. Mayo Clinic Family Health Book Second Edition (New York: William Morrow and Company Inc., 1996), pp. 175-197

How well the newborn adjusts to life depends on genetics, the life experienced in the uterus, the medical care received during labor and delivery and the concern and management it receives as a neonate—the first 28 days of life.[6]

CHAPTER SUMMARY

THE REPRODUCTIVE SYSTEM AND THE CHURCH AS THE WOMB OF THE BODY OF CHRIST:

- When God created man, he built in him a need to love, worship, respect and honor Himself.

- Believers inspire people to become believers by living an exemplary life and assisting them to respond to the call of God on and in their lives. This is the believer's role in spiritual reproduction.

- As the muscle of the uterus expands to accommodate a large baby or multiple babies, so the capacity of the church expands to accommodate added believers.

- Potential believers are to be nurtured and protected as the uterus protects an unborn baby.

- Jesus made provisions for spiritual growth for his followers as the placenta in the uterus provides nourishment for the growth of the fetus.

- Travail, meaning hard work, is required for souls to be born into the Body of Christ, under the anointing of the Holy Spirit. Travail is known as labor for the physical birth process.

- Spiritual birth takes place when a person accepts Jesus' crucifixion and bloodshed as payment for his or her own sins. Physical birth takes place when the baby leaves the uterus and becomes a newborn.

- The Spirit of Christ is in believers from the time they accept him as Savior. When filled with God's Spirit, they inherit his dominant traits, the fruit of the Spirit, similar to the way children inherit the dominant traits of their parents.

PREGNANCY

- Pregnant teens receive less prenatal care than pregnant mature women, but they need more care.

- Pregnant teens are at higher risk of complications not because of age but because of the neglect of themselves.

---

[6] Adele Pillitteri PNA Nursing Care of the Growing Family First Edition (Boston: Little, Brown and Company, 1976), pp. 217

CHAPTER EIGHT
The Integumentary System – Skin

The skin and the organs derived from it, such as hair, nails, glands and specialized receptors, constitute the integumentary system of the body. While the skin appears to be a simple, thin covering that keeps the body together and gives it protection, it is quite complex in structure. This organ helps maintain homeostasis and is essential for the survival of the body.

1. The skin is the largest organ of the body, occupying a surface area of approximately 3,000 square inches.
2. It covers the body and protects the underlying tissues from bacterial invasion, from drying out and from harmful light rays.
3. Skin is composed of four layers in the epidermis, each having a specific function. In areas where exposure to friction is greatest, such as the palms of hands and soles of feet, there is a fifth layer of skin.
4. The dermis is under the epidermis and contains connective tissues with many blood vessels, nerves, glands and hair follicles.
5. One of the ways that skin maintains homeostasis of the body is by controlling body temperature. Man is a warm-blooded organism. This means that he is able to maintain a constant internal body temperature (98.6°F) even though the environmental temperature may vary over a broad range. Let us assume that a person is participating in an athletic event where the temperature is 100°F. A sequence of events is set into operation to counteract this above-normal temperature, which may be considered a stress on the body. Sensing devices in the skin called receptors pick up the stimulus--in this case, heat--and activate nerves that send the message to the brain. A temperature-regulating area of the brain then sends a nerve impulse to the sweat glands in the skin and they produce perspiration. As the perspiration evaporates from the surface of the skin, the skin is cooled, and body temperature is lowered. After the sweat glands are activated, the skin receptors continue to keep the brain informed about the external temperature. The brain, in turn, continues to send messages to the sweat glands until the temperature returns to 98.6°F.
6. Skin receives stimuli from the environment through specialized receptors and sends messages to the brain.[1]

[1] Gerard J. Tortora and Nicholas Anagnostakos, Principles of Anatomy and Physiology (San Francisco: Canfield Press, 1975), pp. 80-84

THE INTEGUMENTARY SYSTEM

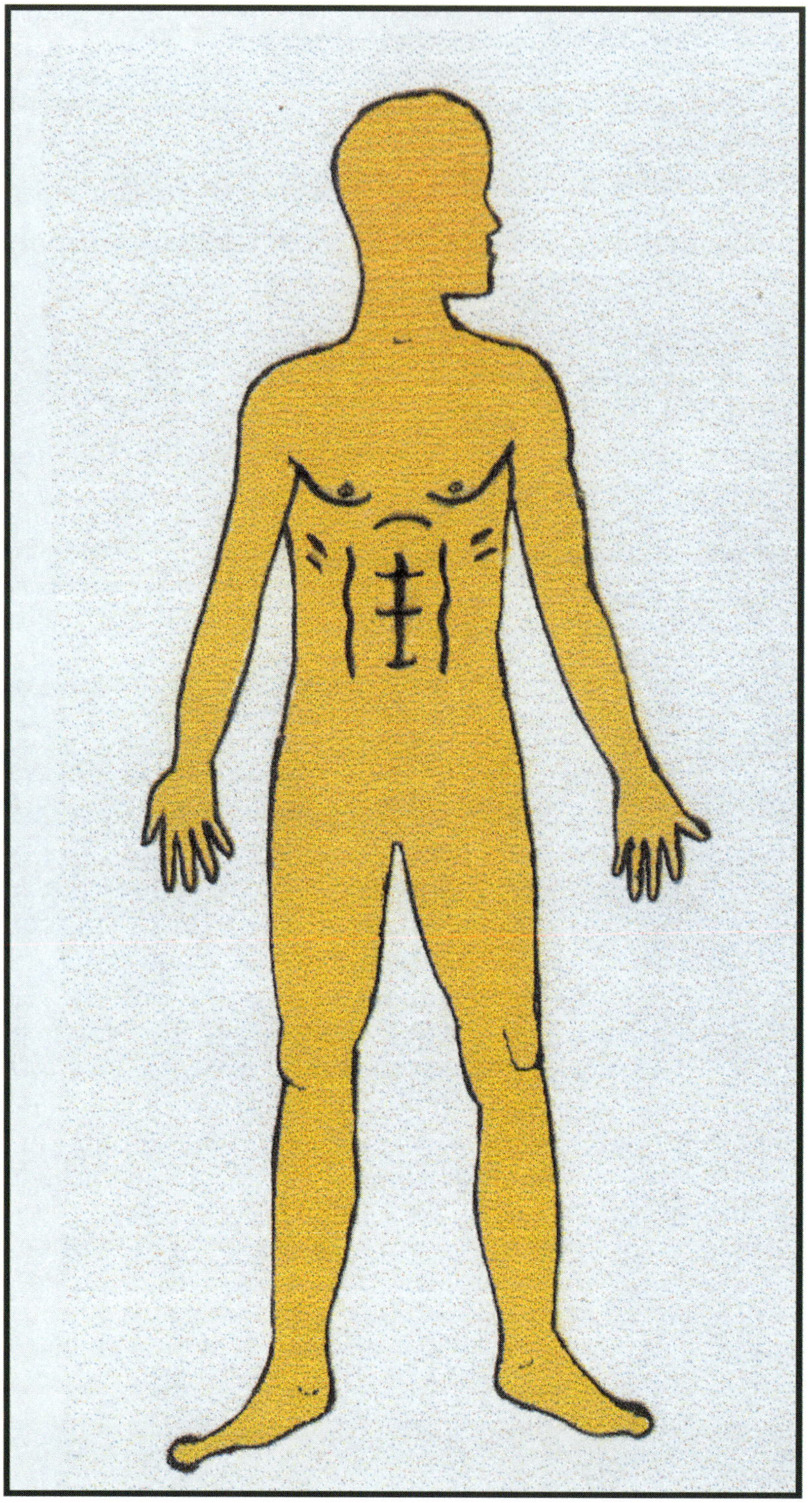

The Skin

Looking closely at the back of your hand using a magnifying glass, you see multiple geometrical shapes touching each other on every side. These shapes change in size and configuration as the fingers are extended and then flexed into a fist. The shapes are less distinct on the skin of the arms, legs, face and abdomen, and depending on the individual there may be a presence or absence of hair and glands. The coloring of the skin varies from one part of the body to the next, and cells on the face are a great distance from those on the feet. Yet, the normal skin is continuous and seamless over the entire body, forming one organ and covering a single body.

THE INTEGUMENTARY SYSTEM
Believers Working Together

The integumentary system encompasses all of the systems of the body: circulatory, digestive, skeletal, muscular, reproductive, nervous, endocrine, respiratory and urinary systems. The writer envisions the integumentary system as a gross illustration of individual human cells with each geometric shape representing a single cell or one of the world's millions of believers. They have visible differences, some close together and in touch with each other while others are tens to thousands of miles apart. Yet the cells form one physical body and believers form one Body of Christ. This panoramic view of the universal Body of Christ enclosed in multiple layers of skin encompasses multiple denominations, faiths and methods. Jesus told his disciples, "And other sheep I have, which are not of this fold: them also I must bring, and they shall hear my voice; and there shall be one fold, and one shepherd." (John 10:16) Although denominations and ministries may differ in their focus of ministry—some specializing in faith teaching or prosperity, others local and foreign missions and so on—all are important for the spiritual growth of believers and ministries of the church, and they are enclosed within the same Body of Christ. "And there are differences of administrations, but the same Lord. And there are diversities of operations, but it is the same God which worketh all in all." (I Corinthians 12:5-6)

A major deficiency in human nature is the tendency to allow differences to separate us and defeat our ability to work together in unity. In all aspects of humanity people find insurmountable reasons for religious differences. The reasons are as shallow as doctrines that include or exclude female ministers and pastors or the presence/absence of charismatic beliefs. People also have major fundamental differences—such as whether or not there is a trinity (God the Father, the Son and the Holy Spirit) and what geographical areas belong to opposing religious groups—that keep them apart.

The subject of believers working together is frequently addressed in the Bible, because it is necessary for the survival of the spiritual church. Believers carry out activities essential to the life of the Body of Christ, as the skin carries out many activities essential to the physical body. Therefore, as Paul wrote to the Philippian church, we must "stand fast in one spirit, with one mind striving together for the faith of the gospel." (Phillippians 1:27b)

Skin covers the body and protects the underlying tissues from bacterial invasion, from drying out and from harmful light rays. Often our hands or other body parts are exposed to bacteria when we go fishing, clean the restroom or clean up after our pets. As long as the skin is intact, it serves as a barrier and does not allow the bacteria we are touching to enter our bodies. Jesus told Peter that the gates of hell would not prevail against the church as long as the members believed that Jesus was the Christ, the Son of the living God. (Matthew 16:15-18) Believers must protect the concept of the gospel of Christ and maintain its continuity, stability and strength by living lives that are consistent with their beliefs. Paul wrote, "I beseech you that ye walk worthy of the vocation wherewith ye are called, with all lowliness and meekness, with longsuffering, forbearing one another in love; Endeavoring to keep the unity of the spirit in the bond of peace." (Ephesians 4:1b-3) "Only let your conversation (way of life) be as it becometh the gospel of Christ." (Phillipians 1:27a) Being a member of the Body of Christ requires caring for and protecing one another. "As we have therefore opportunity, let us do good unto all men, especially unto them who are of the household of faith." (Galatians 6:10)

Skin is composed of multiple layers, each having a specific function. Some of the complexities of the church can be attributed to the fact that as sons and daughters of God, members from variable ethnic, social and financial backgrounds must work together in harmony. In the New Testament church, Paul found that this led to cliques, competition for positions and generally disgruntled members, which hindered the reputation, growth and health of the church. He focused on helping them reason through these interpersonal issues in his letters to the churches at Corinth and Rome by comparing the church to something very familiar to all of them. "The body is a unit, though it is made up of many parts; and though all its parts are many, they form one body. So it is with Christ. For we were all baptized by one Spirit into one body—whether Jews or Greeks, slave or free—and we were all given the one Spirit to drink." (I Corinthians 12:12,13 NIV)

"Now the body is not made up of one part but of many. If the foot should say, 'Because I am not a hand, I do not belong to the body,' it would not for that reason cease to be part of the body. And if the ear should say, 'Because I am not an eye, I do not belong to the body,' it would not for that reason cease to be part of the body. If the whole body were an eye, where would the sense of hearing be, if the whole body were an ear, where would the sense of smell be? But in fact God has arranged the parts in the body, every one of them, just as he wanted them to be. If they were all one part, where would the body be? As it is, there are many parts, but one body.

"The eye cannot say to the hand, 'I don't need you!' And the head cannot say to the feet, 'I don't need you!' On the contrary, those parts of the body that seem to be weaker are indispensable, and the parts that we think are less honorable we treat with special honor. And the parts that are unpresentable are treated with special modesty, while our presentable parts need no special treatment. But God has combined the members of the body and has given greater honor to the parts that lacked it, so that there should be no division in the body, but that its parts should have equal concern for each other." (I Corinthians 12:14-24 NIV)

This excerpt from Corinthians gives believers a glimpse of the big picture, the panoramic view of the Body of Christ, and addresses human interpersonal relationships. It shows first that there is no class system in the church, no discrimination in regard to race or social status. Next, it helps us visualize the senselessness of everyone trying to compete for the same position, rendering the church ineffective and powerless. Considering the word "parts" in the above scripture as though they were denominations and various faiths, there are many denominations and faiths; yet they form one body.

Some churches focus on faith, others on prosperity or ministries. But can the faith church say that there is no purpose for missions? Can the missionary ministries say there is no prosperity in God? If they all had one focus, where would the Body of Christ be? There are mega-churches and storefront churches, and the storefront churches are as honorable as mega-churches. In the Body of Christ, every position is honorable and vital to its purpose and effectiveness in the universe.

The dermis layer of the skin contains connective tissues with many blood vessels, nerves, glands and hair follicles. From the spiritual perspective, there are many gifts in the Body of Christ. To do one's part most effectively requires knowledge of the Word (blood vessels), connection to the spirit of God (nerves), the traits of God (glands) and God's protection (hair follicles). How the believers should be humble and gracious enough to practice their gifts concurrently and effectively with other believers is described again by Paul, utilizing an analogy of the Body of Christ in the following excerpt of scripture:

"For by the grace given me I say to every one of you: *Do not think of yourself more highly than you ought, but rather think of yourself with sober judgment, in accordance with the measure of faith God has given you.* Just as each of us has one body with many members, and these members do not all have the same function, so in Christ we who are many form one body, and each member belongs to all the others. We have different gifts, according to the grace given us. If a man's gift is prophesying, let him use it in proportion to his faith. If it is serving, let him serve; if it is teaching let him teach; if it is encouraging, let him encourage; if it is contributing to the needs of others, let him give generously; if it is leadership, let him govern diligently; if it is showing mercy, let him do it cheerfully." (Romans 12:3-8 NIV) Paul is telling the Romans that they must do an honest self-assessment and whatever the gift, position or task a believer accepts or is used by God to do, it must be done well and according to the spiritual level to which the believer has grown. There is a synergy in the gifts of the spirit that contributes to the effectiveness of the Body of Christ.

Consider the word "members" in the above scripture as though they were various churches and denominations. Just as the Body of Christ has many churches and denominations, they do not all have the same function, focus or gift, yet they form one body, and each church belongs to all the others. Whatever the specialty, each church must do it well and to the honor of God. Here, too, there must be a synergy among churches, causing them to spiritually enhance the effects of one another.

Every cell in a healthy physical body fulfills its function or it is considered diseased. When a diseased cell multiplies, it forms infections and tumors, causing pain, and without an intervention, leads to death. "These six things doth the Lord hate: yea, seven are an abomination unto him: A proud look, a lying tongue, and hands that shed innocent blood, An heart that deviseth wicked imaginations, feet that be swift in running to mischief, A false witness that speaketh lies, and he that soweth discord among brethren." (Proverbs 6:16-19) These actions, when performed by church members, are like cancers in the Body of Christ, leading to the destruction of members and Christ's cause for the church.

Skin maintains homeostasis of the body by controlling body temperature, preventing excessive loss of inorganic and organic materials, and excreting water and salts. Homeostasis, meaning balance and harmony, requires commitment and spiritual connection within the Body of Christ. The description of the physiology involved in maintaining a constant physical body temperature shows that messages are sent to and from the brain in a sequence of events. This system of monitoring gives instant feedback between the brain and the cells that regulates the internal environment of the body to keep it harmonious within. Similarly, believers must communicate with God to temper their actions so that there is absolute balance and harmony in the Body of Christ. Paul told the members of the church in Rome, "Love must be sincere. Hate what is evil; cling to what is good. Be devoted to one another in brotherly love. Honor one another above yourselves. Never be lacking in zeal, but keep your spiritual fervor, serving the Lord. Be joyful in hope, patient in affliction, faithful in prayer. Share with God's people who are in need. Practice hospitality.

"Bless those who persecute you; bless and do not curse. Rejoice with those who rejoice; mourn with those who mourn. Live in harmony with one another. Do not be proud, but be willing to associate with people of low position. Do not be conceited. If it is possible, as far as it depends on you, live at peace with everyone." (Romans 12:9-16,18NIV) These traits are the fruit of the Spirit of God that is given believers just for the asking and are described in Chapter Ten.

Skin receives stimuli from the environment via receptors. The ability of the skin to receive stimuli from the environment means the receptors in the skin tell the brain what is going on outside the body that may impact the internal body. Occurrences and trends in the community should be communicated to God through prayer, so that he can direct the church to intervene effectively with a positive outcome for the community.

When members of the Body of Christ become aware of incidents that occur in their local church or at another location of believers that may impact the effectiveness of the church on the community, it is time to pray to God through Christ, who is the head of the church. Believers must remember their need for each other and, as told by James, the brother of Jesus, "Therefore confess your sins (faults) to each other and pray for each other so that you may be healed. The prayer of a righteous man is powerful and effective." (James 5:16 NIV)

A glimpse of the **PANORAMIC** view of the Body of Christ: If the effectiveness of a church is measured by the extent to which it carries out Jesus' purpose and fulfills the ministries of the church, imagine this: What if in a coordinated effort, each church in Anytown, USA, targeted an at risk group in the community: homeless, school dropouts, elderly, hospice, various support groups, abused children and adults, substance abusers, pregnant teens, HIV-AIDS patients, inmates in jail etc. What if each church took its group under its wing and visited, prayed for and with, taught, fed, encouraged and nurtured that group toward Christ?

The outcome would be a city in which the Body of Christ worked together within the covering of one continuous and seamless body, having the same purpose and with the same spirit, for the cause of Christ. And, if this process took place in every city in the world, the impact would be phenomenal, and Jesus' charge to His disciples would be implemented. "Verily, verily, I say unto you, He that believeth on me, the works that I do shall he do also; and greater works than these shall he do; because I go unto my father.

And whatsoever ye shall ask in my name, that will I do, that the Father may be glorified in the Son." (John 14:12-13) There could be no chance for failure.

THE INTEGUMENTARY SYSTEM ■ PATHOLOGY
Cancer

What is Cancer?

There are many types of cancer, and it always consists of uncontrolled growth and spread of abnormal cells. Some cancers can affect one organ, while others are more generalized. Normal cells are created by cell division,[2] and different types of cells having special functions are created in a normal process called cell differentiation. Cell division and differentiation are a patterned, orderly fashion of growth and development. Cancer cells lack the controls that stop or switch off growth, so they divide without constraint, moving normal cells aside and affecting their normal function and growth. Cancer cells compete with normal cells for space and nutrition. Uncontrolled cancer cells can grow into a mass called a tumor and destroy nearby cells. Cancer cells can also migrate to other parts of the body by traveling with blood or through the lymph system to other parts of the body. This process is called metastasis.[3]

Causes of Cancer

Cancer is caused by external factors (chemicals, radiation and viruses) and by internal factors (hormones, immune and metabolic conditions and inherited mutations). Some of these factors are avoidable; others are not.

Cancer Warning Signs

According to the American Cancer Society, if you have any of these seven warning signs, consult your physician immediately:

1. Change in bowel or bladder habits
2. Sore that does not heal
3. Unusual bleeding or discharge
4. Thickening or lump in a breast or elsewhere in your body
5. Indigestion or swallowing difficulty
6. Obvious change in a wart or mole
7. Nagging cough or hoarseness

Cancer Diagnosis

When we take advantage of the cancer screening procedures available today, many cancers can be detected early enough to be cured. Mammograms, stool samples and PSA blood tests are some of the common screening procedures. Early detection and diagnosis increases the chances for cancer to be treated before it spreads to other organs and tissues in the body.

---

[2] See Illustration of Cell division, Page Two.

[3] David E. Larson, MD Mayo Clinic Family Health Book Second Edition (New York: William Morrow & Co. Inc., 1996), pp. 1290-1299

Identifying the type and location of the cancer helps physicians determine its characteristics such as rate of growth, the tendency to spread and the organs to which it is likely to spread. This enables the physician to plan the appropriate treatment program, which will be different for each case.

Types of Cancer Treatment

Surgery-to remove the cancerous growth, relieve an obstruction or to determine if malignant cells have spread to other parts of the body.
Radiation-high doses of X-ray aimed at cancer cells to destroy them;
Chemotherapy-use of medication to destroy cancer cells.
Immunotherapy-the use of biologic agents to help the body's immune system fight cancer cells as foreign cells.
Lasers-high intensity light aimed at cancer cells.
T Cells-normal cells in our body that fight cancer. Researchers hope to remove some T Cells from the body, stimulate their growth and return them to the body in large numbers to fight cancer cells.

THE INTEGUMENTARY SYSTEM ♥ HEALTH & WELLNESS
Cancer Remission & Prevention

REMISSION

One is in a state of remission when there is no clinical evidence, no symptoms of disease. During this time, the treatment in certain cancers is continued or intensified because cancer cells are still present even when there are no symptoms. Once the cells are completely gone, there may be a final phase of maintenance treatment for two or three more years, when new drugs are given intermittently.[4]

PREVENTION

There are precautions that we can take to avoid the risk of cancer, yet there are no guarantees. The following guidelines will assist in reducing the controllable risks:

Tobacco Use

Smoking is responsible for almost 90 percent of all deaths from lung cancer and for about 30 percent of all cancer deaths.[5] Those who use smokeless tobacco are at increased risk of cancer of the mouth, throat, larynx or esophagus.

---

[4] McCance, Huether Pathophysiology the Biologic Basis for Disease in Adults and Children Third Edition, (St. Louis: Mosby, 1998), pp. 961

[5] David E. Larson M.D. Mayo Clinic Family Health Book Second Edition, (New York: William Morrow and Company Inc., 1996), pp. 1294

Sun Exposure

If you are light skinned, you should limit your exposure to the sun and use a sun blocker, too. Children playing in the sun also need sun blocker. Studies have shown that darker skinned individuals are not exempt from skin cancer.

Alcohol

Heavy drinkers are at increased risk of cancer of the mouth, larynx, throat, esophagus or liver.

Menopause Treatments

Physicians often prescribe estrogen for women to treat the symptoms of menopause and to prevent osteoporosis. Estrogen, however, poses certain risks of endometrial cancer, so its benefits and risks should be discussed and weighed with your physician.

Radiation Exposure

Exposure to X-ray radiation in excess increases the risk of cancer. Although most medical X-rays are adjusted to give the lowest dose possible, there still could be a risk of radon in your home with the potential of exposure.

Nutrition

Your risk of cancer may be enhanced by what you eat. Diets high in fats or salt-cured, smoked or nitrite-cured foods may be potentially hazardous, while foods high in fiber and rich in vitamins A and C may help lower your risk for certain cancers.[6]

REALITY CHECK:

In the realm of the church, some members fail to focus on the Word and the purpose of the church, promoting their personal agendas instead. When these members cause others to lose focus also, the result is a destructive effect similar to cancer in the physical body—spiritual malnutrition, weakness and potential spiritual death--for other members. The treatment is for believers to continuously apply the discipline of the Word of God to their lives, even when it seems they have reached a comfortable level of spiritual maturity. Sin, like cancer in a state of remission, has the potential to revive and spread if it is not monitored and treated long term with the Word of God.

---

[6] Ibid., pp. 1290-1299

CHAPTER SUMMARY

THE INTEGUMENTARY SYSTEM GIVES A PANORAMIC VIEW OF THE BODY OF CHRIST:

There are many geometric shapes in the skin, each similar to a human cell. These shapes or cells illustrate believers in the body of Christ in several ways:

1. Some are close enough together to touch,while others are far apart.

2. They have varied sizes, shapes, coloration and purposes.

3. The normal skin is continuous and seamless over the entire body.

4. Skin, like believers in the Body of Christ, forms one organ and covers one single body.

The analogy of skin and believers stresses the importance of diversity and respect between them whether in close proximity or far apart. Paul made an accurate visualization of the spiritual Body of Christ to stress the need for cooperation between believers by comparing it to the physical body.

1. Skin protects the body from infection as believers protect the integrity of the gospel of Christ.

2. Paul told believers that the Body of Christ is made up of many parts, as is the physical body, each having its own purpose and function.

3. Believers fighting and competing for the same position and function in the church cause the spiritual body of Christ to be ineffective and powerless, as a physical body would be if it were just an ear or eye.

4. As skin maintains homeostasis in the body, so balance and harmony are maintained in the Body of Christ via the believers' spiritual connection to God.

5. Positions accepted in the Body of Christ must be fulfilled optimally, as cells in our physical bodies do to maintain a state of health.

CANCER

Cancer cells are created during the time that cells are changing from basic cells into specialized cells, and they lack the controls that cause them to stop growing.

CHAPTER NINE
The Nervous System

The nervous system controls all activities of the body by electrical impulses. When electrical impulses are not properly connected in the body, the body has little to no movement or evidence of life. This chapter will focus on the two major divisions in the nervous system: The central nervous system that includes the brain and spinal cord and the peripheral nervous system that includes the nerves that connect the brain and spinal cord to all parts of the body.

The Central Nervous System

- Governs posture and muscular movements—*fine* movements such as writing and *gross* movements such as walking.

- Interprets incoming sensory information such as smell, hearing, sight, taste and speech. It recognizes the size, shape, weight, temperature and texture of objects.

- Controls emotions and intellect—memory, reasoning, will, personality traits and judgment.

- Responds quickly to stimuli that upset the internal environment to control homeostasis.

The Peripheral Nervous System

- The Somatic System is responsible for all movements in which conscious control plays a part.
    - Sensory nerve fibers run from the skeletal muscles, skin and internal organs to the spinal cord and brain.
    - Motor nerve fibers run from the brain and spinal cord to all skeletal muscles.
    - Some nerve fibers are combined into networks called plexuses (meaning braids) that supply general regions of the body. The brachial plexus supplies the skin and muscles of the arms and hands, the ribs and the abdominal wall.

- A Somatic Reflex is movement of skeletal muscle caused by a nerve arc that goes between a muscle and the spinal cord without brain involvement. A classic example is the "knee jerk" the doctor elicits when a tap below the knee makes the leg jerk. This test evaluates the continuity of the nerve connection.[1]

Each cell of the body has a direct line of communication with the brain via nerve fibers that run between cells, the spinal cord and the brain. This communication link is an

---

[1] Gerard J. Tortora and Nicholas Anagnostakos, Principles of Anatomy and Physiology (San Francisco: Canfield Press, 1975), pp. 228-272

impulse or stimulus that runs up and down the nerve fiber in an instant similar to a bolt of lightning in a thunderstorm.

THE NERVOUS SYSTEM

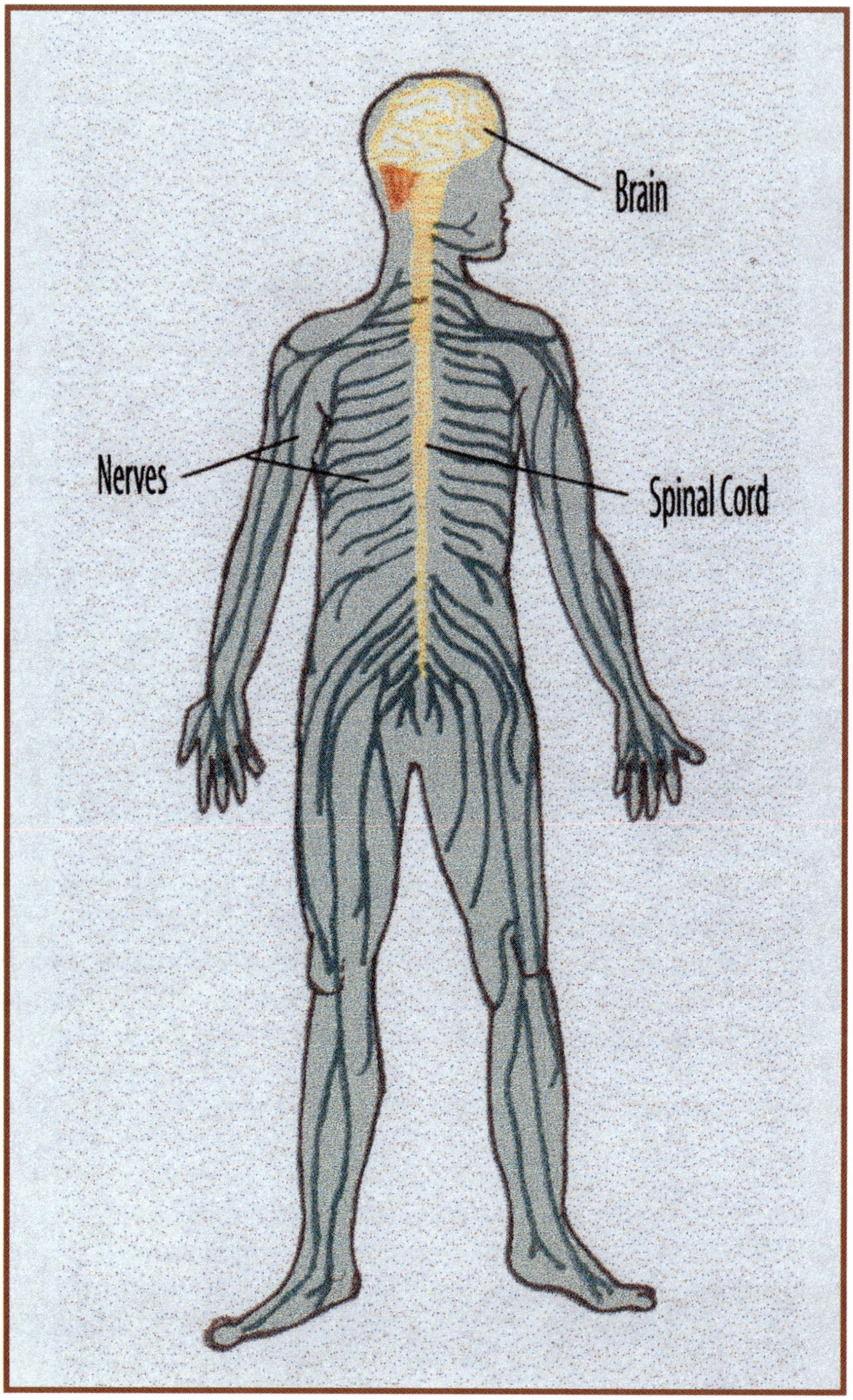

The Brain, Spinal Cord and Peripheral Nerves

THE NERVOUS SYSTEM: **The Spiritual Godhead**

God the Father, Jesus the Son and the Holy Spirit form the Godhead of the spiritual church. The brain, spinal cord and peripheral nerves form the nervous system of the physical body. The Godhead is the life of the church and controls all of its activities, just as the nervous system controls the life and all activities of the physical body.

In the Body of Christ, a direct line of communication extends between the believer and God through Jesus via the Holy Spirit, which is comparable to nerve fibers connecting the brain to the cells of the body. The in dwelling of the Holy Spirit is God's Spirit emanating from Himself into the life of the believer. This occurs after the believer is redeemed—born again, in atonement—during liturgical service or during penance. Within moments, hours or even years after being born again, when believers ask, God's Holy Spirit connects with the Spirit of Christ that is in believers from the time of salvation (DNA in Chapter One). Having the indwelling of the Holy Spirit is vital in the process of living a consecrated life, communicating with God and having the power to carry out His will. Jesus said, "But the Comforter, which is the Holy Ghost, whom the Father will send in my name, he shall teach you all things, and bring all things to your remembrance, whatsoever I have said unto you." (John 14:26)

God gave his son to be sacrificed for the sin of humanity, the process described in Chapter Seven. Because Jesus shed his blood and paid the penalty for sin, there is forgiveness, hope and deliverance for all. Having completed this portion of God's plan, Jesus, who was God in the flesh, was buried, conquered death, hell and the grave, rose again and now sits at the right hand of God the Father. The apostle Paul writes that Jesus actually existed in the beginning with God and has now been appointed by God to be the head and supreme leader of His people in the new dispensation of grace. "He is the image of the invisible God, the firstborn over all creation. For by him all things were created: things in heaven and on earth, visible and invisible, whether thrones or powers or rulers or authorities; all things were created by him and for him. He is before all things, and in him all things hold together. And he is the head of the body, the church; he is the beginning and the firstborn from among the dead, so that in everything he might have the supremacy " (Colossians 1:15-18 NIV)

God worked out his divine plan for mankind by appointing his son, Jesus, to be the CEO, head and brains of the organized system of people who believe on him. To access the presence of God and His benefits, Jesus told his disciple Thomas, "I am the way, the truth and the life: no man cometh unto the Father, but by me." (John 14:6) "For God was pleased to have all his fullness dwell in him (Jesus), and through him to reconcile to himself all things, whether things on earth or things in heaven, by making peace through his blood, shed on the cross." (Colossians 1:19,20NIV) The spirit of Christ engulfs a person's spirit when he or she believes, confesses having lived a sinful life and accepts the blood that Christ shed on the cross as the payment for his or her personal sins. The Spirit of God identifies and connects with the Spirit of Christ within the believer, and thus the original relationship between God and man is restored.

*The **Central Nervous System** controls emotions and intellect – memory, reasoning, will, personality traits and judgment.* The Spirit of God guides believers—to the extent of the will of the individual—controlling his/her emotions, intellect, memory, reasoning, personality traits and judgment. When believers allow, God's spiritual traits become dominant in their lives and transform them into a new being. The change that takes place in fully committed believers is sometimes described as a 180 degree turn, in which they acquire an entirely new personality. It can only occur when we submit our own will, reasoning and personality to God (making them recessive traits) and allow His spiritual traits to dominate. In the Bible, Matthew tells of a man with an unclean spirit who lived in the graveyard and was so wild that no one could control him even with chains. He cried out and cut himself with stones night and day. But after an encounter with Jesus, men observed him sitting, clothed and in his right mind. (Mark 5:1-15) This was indeed a new personality.

*The **Central Nervous System** governs posture and muscular movements, both fine movements used for writing and gross movements such as walking*. Whereas under the dispensation of the law in the Old Testament, God's people were led by the laws of the Ten Commandments and followed various rituals, the New Testament introduces the dispensation of grace—an era in which God leads his people by His Spirit. "For this is the covenant that I will make with the house of Israel after those days, saith the Lord; I will put my laws into their mind and write them in their hearts: and I will be to them a God, and they shall be to me a people: And they shall not teach every man his neighbour, and every man his brother, saying, know the Lord: for all shall know me, from the least to the greatest." (Hebrews 8:10,11) We no longer need to go through someone else to know God, we can go to Him ourselves. God's spirit is imprinted into the mind and conscience of believers, forming a one on one relationship, regardless of worldly status, power, wealth, ethnicity, gender or previous behavior.

God has postured the church to be the moral and spiritual standard for the world. In his Word, He sets a pattern for the lifestyle of believers. "For ye are the temple of the living God; as God hath said, I will dwell in them, and walk in them; and I will be their God and they shall be my people. Wherefore come out from among them, and be ye separate, saith the Lord, and touch not the unclean thing." (II Corinthians 6:16b-17a). Believers stand apart, stand tall and walk tall.

*The **Central Nervous System** Interprets incoming sensory stimuli (information), recognizing the size, shape, weight, temperature and texture of objects*. When touching fabric without seeing it, for instance, we know by the texture and weight of the material when we are touching silk versus denim; or corduroy versus satin, because the brain interprets the texture and weight of the material. Similarly on a spiritual level, Jesus knows our feelings, needs, weaknesses and shortcomings. In the letter to the Hebrews, the writer wrote, "For we do not have a high priest who is unable to sympathize with our weaknesses, but we have one who has been tempted in every way, just as we are--yet was without sin. Let us then approach the throne of grace with confidence, so that we may receive mercy and find grace to help us in our time of need." (Hebrews 4:15-16 NIV)

A strong weapon that Satan uses against believers is their lack of assurance that God hears or cares about them. When feeling this void, believers are vulnerable to temptation. A simple exercise to practice to overcome this state of mind is to focus—think about a scripture that is significant to you or just your need. With closed eyes stroke the surface of a table, a piece of fabric, any object and sense the temperature, texture, flexibility, odor and listen for sounds. The ability to identify the characteristics of the surface or object touched is the result of the brain interpreting the information coming to it from the fingertips. This is your reminder and reassurance that as a cell in the Body of Christ, Jesus is connected to you and is aware of your feelings, hears you when you call and is sensitive to your needs and weaknesses.

John, the beloved disciple, wrote about Jesus' friend Lazarus and how Jesus was emotionally touched by the tears of Lazarus' friends and loved ones. When his sisters told Jesus about his illness and then his death, Jesus went to the cemetery with them and saw their grief and felt the pain of the family and friends. "When Jesus therefore saw her weeping, and the Jews also weeping which came with her, he groaned in the spirit, and was troubled, And said, Where have ye laid him? They said unto him, Lord, come and see. *Jesus wept*. Then said the Jews, Behold how he loved him!" (John 11:33-36) Then Jesus called Lazarus' name, and Lazarus came from the grave.

The ***Central Nervous System*** *responds quickly to stimuli that upset the internal environment, to control homeostasis.* The nervous system regulates homeostasis—harmony in the body—by detecting when it is headed out of its balanced state and sends messages to the proper organs to counteract the stress. When the brain receives the message that it is very hot outside, it knows that this could be a threat to the health and wellness of the physical body. It sends messages to the sweat glands to release water onto the surface of the skin, and as the sweat evaporates, the body is cooled. The brain also sends messages to decrease blood sugar when we eat candy and to release carbon dioxide when we exert the body during exercise.

The Spirit of God, the common bond that is shared among believers, senses when the Body of Christ is headed out of its balanced state. It causes believers to adjust their attitudes, tone of voice, priorities and even plans that could cause a risk or threat to the spiritual wellbeing of others or the spiritual church. Thus the importance of keeping one's mind spiritually tuned. "Let this mind be in you, which was also in Christ Jesus." (Philippians 2:5) So that, "When the enemy shall come in like a flood, the Spirit of the Lord shall lift up a standard against him." (Isaiah 59:19b)

The Somatic portion of the ***Peripheral Nervous System*** *is responsible for all movements in which there is some conscious control.* This is the part of the nervous system that connects the brain to the muscles and cells of the body via sensory and motor nerves and is responsible for two-way communications. Nerves, like phone wires, carry information that gives us assurance of the presence of another and conveys messages to and from the caller.

When Jesus knew that he would be leaving his disciples, he said, "And I will ask the Father, and he will give you another counselor, to be with you forever—the spirit of truth. The world cannot accept him, because it neither sees him nor knows him. But you know him, for he lives with you and shall be in you. I will not leave you as orphans; I will come to you." (John 14:16-18 NIV) Jesus was speaking of the Holy Spirit that would convey His presence to the disciples after He returned to heaven. Just as the disciples felt strong, confident and capable when Jesus was with them, they would be powerful in His absence because the Holy Spirit would guide and direct them. "But ye shall receive power, after that the Holy Ghost is come upon you: and ye shall be witnesses unto me both in Jerusalem, and in all Judaea, and in Samaria, and unto the uttermost part of the earth. And when he had spoken these things, while they beheld, he was taken up: and a cloud received him out of their sight." (Acts 1:8,9)

Sensory nerve fibers carry information from the muscles, skin and internal organs through the spinal cord to the brain. Sensory information: sight, smell, touch, sound and taste comes from receiving cells in the skin, muscles and internal organs i.e. the stomach, liver or bladder, and instantly travels up the spinal cord to the brain. The Holy Spirit carries messages we send to Jesus via our prayers; then it carries the answer back. Solomon, the wisest man on earth, told us, "Trust in the Lord with all thine heart; and lean not unto thine own understanding. In all thy ways acknowledge him (send prayer up), and he shall direct thy paths (the answer returns)." (Proverbs 3:5,6)

Motor nerve fibers carry messages from the brain and spinal cord to all skeletal muscles, skin and internal organs. Instructions from the brain tell the muscles of the hand to move away from the fire quickly, to tiptoe past a sleeping rottweiler or to run out of the path of a speeding car. Jesus' response to our prayers may come from him via a sermon or lesson from the minister, while reading a daily scripture passage, in a dream, as a thought while driving, or as a prophecy from a believer. The Psalmist said, "The steps of a good man are ordered by the Lord." (Psalm 37:23a)

Motor nerve fibers that are inactivated due to an interruption in the electrical flow of information will not carry messages from the brain to the body, telling it to move away from danger. Believers who continuously send messages to the Lord but do not take time to listen to or carry out the instructions he sends have the characteristics of one with a motor nerve dysfunction. The Body of Christ is most effective when the Holy Spirit is in place and like the sensory and motor nerves make it possible for believers to send, then receive and obey the messages from God. "Jesus replied, "If anyone loves me, he will obey my teaching. My Father will love him, and we will come to him and make our home with him." (John 14:23 NIV)

Plexus networks *consist of many nerve fibers that are bundled together to supply general regions of the body*. For instance, the brachial plexus controls the arm, wrist, hand, ribs and abdominal wall. This characteristic of the Peripheral Nervous System brings us to the concept of regions of cells serviced by bundles of nerve fibers sending and receiving messages to and from a general area of the body. The brain is still the destination for ascending messages and the origin of descending messages.

When members of the Body of Christ unite with one purpose and on one accord, the Holy Spirit within them unites to form a plexus through which God can orchestrate mighty feats. "Where two or three are gathered together in my name, there am I in the midst of them." (Matthew 18:20) There is a spiritual dimension experienced in a group setting that adds depth and spirituality to one's life. Spirit filled participants coming together form a powerful presence of God's Spirit like an electrical substation. When they begin to worship God for who He is and praise him for what He has done, believers and non-believers experience the completeness and power of the Godhead in the congregation. "Yet a time is coming and has now come when the true worshipers will worship the Father in spirit and truth, for they are the kind of worshipers the Father seeks. God is spirit, and his worshipers must worship in spirit and in truth." (John 4:23-24)

There are many forms and formats for a church service, but they have several common elements. *Songs* employ the intriguing effects of music and words that express admiration and praises to God, while soothing and stimulating the spirit deep inside of participants. *Prayers* express devotion, needs and desires, while asking God for strength and forgiveness. There is an opportunity to give an *offering* so that everyone can help finance the work of the ministry of the church and obey God's instructions to give tithes and offerings. And finally, a *message* from God to warn, encourage or instruct those in attendance. Whatever the format, participants should leave a church service knowing that they have been lifted, motivated, healed, received understanding, insight or a solution. While some people take notes, others highlight verses in their Bibles to help retain information to "digest" in the days ahead. All should have connected spiritually with God in some way during the worship service, resulting in an enhanced life that is quickened spiritually, emotionally and/or physically.

Throughout the worship service, believers not only receive. They offer themselves to be used by the Holy Spirit in whatever capacity God needs. "But yield yourselves unto God, as those that are alive from the dead, and your members as instruments of righteousness unto God." (Romans 6:13b) There are several ways in which God may choose to manifest himself through spirit filled believers during the worship service or at other times to help, enlighten and/or spark the faith of potential and current believers through the *gifts* of the Spirit (See the summary of spiritual gifts, page 90).

The Somatic Reflex involves movement of a muscle from a nerve arc without involving the brain. When a health professional taps a patient just below the knee with a blunt instrument, the leg swings out. A tap on the Achilles tendon just above the heel makes the foot jerk, and a tap near the outer elbow makes the long finger twitch. These muscle movements occur without a stimulus from the brain, as is necessary for voluntary muscle movement. The tests are significant indicators of the condition of nerves as they enter and leave the spinal cord.

Spiritually, believers must develop some reflexes relative to the word that involve obedience to basic guidelines given in the Ten Commandments (Exodus 20:1-17) the Beatitudes of Jesus' Sermon on the Mount (Matthew 5:3-12) and various dos and don'ts that are spelled out in the Bible. For example, there are scriptures that tell us not to kill physically or emotionally, not to render evil for evil, to tell the truth, to be slow to anger and quick to forgive, to have love one for another and many other directives. Once the believer becomes conditioned to respond automatically in these instances, he/she will have formed a reflex response to many of the snares of life that causes some to fall. These are situations that are clearly defined by God and do not require that we ask for guidance, only the will to obey.

GIFT TYPE	GIFT IDENTITY	GIFT DESCRIPTION
GIFTS TO KNOW	• Knowledge (I Kings 19:12) • Wisdom (I Corinthians 12:8) • Discerning of Spirits (Acts 8:23)	• Facts placed in the believer's mind by a superior act of God. • Correct application of facts given by knowledge. • Supernatural revelation of what spirit is in operation, whether good or bad.
POWER or ACTION GIFTS	• Healing (Mark16:15-18) • Miracles (Acts 19:11;16:26) • Faith Hebrews 11:1)	• Supernatural healing of diseases and infirmities, both physical and emotional. • Mighty feats beyond the power of man. • Assurance of answered prayer before it happens.
GIFTS OF COMMUNICATION	• Divers Tongues (I Corinthians 14:2) • Interpretation of Tongues (I Corinthians 12:10) • Prophecy (I Corinthians 14:5) (I Corinthians 14:14)	• God using man to speak earthly and heavenly things. • Translation/interpretation of Tongues. • Message from God without Tongues or interpretation.

Table 3. A brief summary of spiritual gifts

Spinal Cord Trauma

The spinal cord is composed of long nerve fibers leading from the brain that connect to nerves from the skin and muscles. Spinal cord trauma is usually the result of traffic or industrial accidents, gunshot wounds, falls or sports injuries. The injury may result from the spinal cord being pulled and torn—when your chin strikes the steering wheel during a traffic accident; cut—by a knife, metal or bone fragments or a bullet wound; compressed—caused by a car or motorcycle accident; or pushed sideways—by bleeding into or around the spinal cord. Injuries of the spinal cord in the neck area may result when the neck is snapped sharply while playing football, from a shallow-water dive or from a motor vehicle accident.

The immediate effect of a spinal cord injury is often paralysis or loss of sensation in a portion of your body. The part of the body affected by the trauma depends on the level at which the injury occurs in the spinal cord. Body function will be impaired from the level of the injury and below. For instance, a lower back (lumbar) injury can affect bodily functions from the waist down, paralyzing the legs, destroying bowel and bladder control as well as sexual function. This condition is known as *paraplegia*. A neck injury affects the spinal cord at a higher level and may paralyze the muscles used for breathing and the movements of the arms in addition to the functions lost by a paraplegic. This injury resulting in loss of function of all four limbs is called *quadriplegia.*

Spinal cord injuries are very serious and can be fatal if a neck injury stops one's breathing. Physicians usually delay giving a diagnosis of permanent damage for a few days after an accident to allow nerves to recover as swelling subsides. When appropriate, there will be surgical intervention to stabilize the spine, remove bone or foreign objects and release accumulated fluids. Bleeding into the spinal cord can cause some permanent loss of sensation with muscle weakness. Bleeding and accumulation of fluid outside the spinal cord compresses the nerves. In these cases, loss of sensation and muscle function may be temporary, and there will be a dramatic improvement when the swelling subsides or the fluid accumulation is removed surgically.

Following a spinal cord injury, one may expect a long hospitalization for injuries to heal and possibly months of specialized rehabilitation. In the cases of quadriplegia and paraplegia, there are usually recurrent bladder infections, constipation and the potential of burns and other injuries of any part of the body that has loss of sensation. Any impairment remaining after six months will probably be permanent.

Most cuts and other severe forms of trauma to the spinal cord will cause permanent disability or paralysis because nerve fibers seldom rebuild.[2]

---

[2] David E. Larson, M.D. Mayo Clinic Family Health Book Second Edition (New York: William Morrow and Company Inc., 1996), pp. 506-508

Safety Precautions

Accidents occur in seconds and have the potential to permanently change our lives. The pain and suffering caused by simple negligence or a thoughtless deed are staggering, sometimes leading to divorce and mental illness due to blaming self or others.

- Seat belts in vehicles are a must for children, drivers and passengers. Car seats are the law for children of specific age and weight classifications in most states.
- Small children can drown in the five-gallon buckets used for washing the family vehicle.
- Monitor the temperature of hot water to avoid scalding incidents in bath water for children and elderly.
- Throw rugs are tripping hazards for the elderly.
- Use protective equipment when skateboarding, riding bikes and roller-skating to guard the head, elbows and knees.
- Long swinging cords for adjusting window blinds are hanging hazards for children.
- Cleaning chemicals stored in the bathroom and kitchen are poisonous when ingested by children.
- Toddlers require 100% attention when in the tub, near open bodies of water and when playing outdoors.
- Candles and incense should be monitored closely while burning.
- Padding in household furniture allows embers from cigarettes and fireplaces to smolder for hours before flames begin.
- Improper use of extension cords may cause fire. Follow the manufacturer's recommendations.
- Biohazard concerns require that we pay attention to our mail, not opening envelopes that have no return address or those whose handwriting you do not recognize.
- Cell phones have proven to be an important tool for roadside assistance.

CHAPTER SUMMARY

THE NERVOUS SYSTEM IS TO THE BODY WHAT THE GODHEAD IS TO THE SPIRITUAL CHURCH:

- The Nervous System consists of the brain, spinal cord and nerves, while the Godhead is God the Father, Jesus the Son and the Holy Spirit.
- As the body cannot move if the Nervous System is not properly connected, the church cannot move in the spiritual realm or impact the community if its members are not connected to God through Christ and the Holy Spirit.
- The Central Nervous System (CNS) governs posture and muscular movements of the body. God has postured the church to be the moral and spiritual standard for the world and determines the moves that the church should make.
- As the CNS interprets information coming from the body, Jesus interprets and understands our feelings, needs and shortcomings.
- God's spirit is the common element that believers share, making them members of the Body of Christ. It promotes harmony among members as the CNS promotes balance and harmony in our physical bodies.
- A network of nerves called a plexus carries messages to and from a group of cells at once. Groups of believers form a powerful presence of the Spirit of God, which is the ideal environment for petitioning God for needs and receiving special blessings.
- Willing obedience to God's basic commandments is the spiritual counterpart of a reflex arc in the physical body.

SPINAL CORD TRAUMA

- Spinal cord trauma is the result of traffic or industrial accidents, gunshot wounds, falls and sports injuries.
- The level of the injury to the spinal column and the type of injury determine the area of the body that will be temporarily impaired or permanently paralyzed.

HOUSEHOLD SAFETY

- Preplanning and simple precautions can prevent most accidents that occur in the home.

CHAPTER TEN
The Endocrine System

This and the next two chapters will be about systems of the body that maintain homeostasis. They keep the systems reviewed in chapters three through nine in balance and harmony. While the nervous system controls bodily functions through electrical impulses, the endocrine organs affect bodily activities by releasing chemical messengers—hormones—into the bloodstream. The nervous and endocrine systems coordinate their activities like an interlocking super-system. Certain parts of the nervous system routinely stimulate or block the release of hormones. The hormones, in turn, are quite capable of stimulating or blocking the flow of particular nerve impulses. The two systems are interactive.

Endocrine glands of the body are the pituitary, thyroid, parathyroids, adrenals, pancreas, ovaries, testes, pineal and thymus. They are located in various places in the body and secrete hormones into the space between cells, to be absorbed into the cells. Hormones maintain homeostasis of the body by changing the life giving activities of cells. Some of the life functions controlled by hormones are growth, blood-sugar level and reproductive functions.

The endocrine glands function as follows:

- The Pituitary Gland regulates so many body activities that it has been nicknamed the master gland. It is stimulated by the brain and is responsible for bodily activities from growth to reproduction.
- The Thyroid Gland controls the rate of the body's metabolism, causing it to break down protein for energy or to use it for tissue growth.
- The Parathyroid Glands control the rate at which calcium is absorbed into the bones and phosphate is eliminated in urine.
- The Adrenal Glands help control electrolyte balance and blood pressure, provide resistance to stress and produce anti-inflammatories.
- The Pancreas produces glucagon and insulin, which regulate blood sugar.
- The Ovaries and Testes secrete hormones that maintain the sexual characteristics of males and females.
- The Pineal Gland inhibits ovarian function.
- The Thymus Gland is active in antibody production.[1]

---

[1] Gerard J. Tortora and Nicholas Anagnostakos, Principles of Anatomy and Physiology (San Francisco: Canfield Press, 1975), pp. 313-331

THE ENDOCRINE SYSTEM

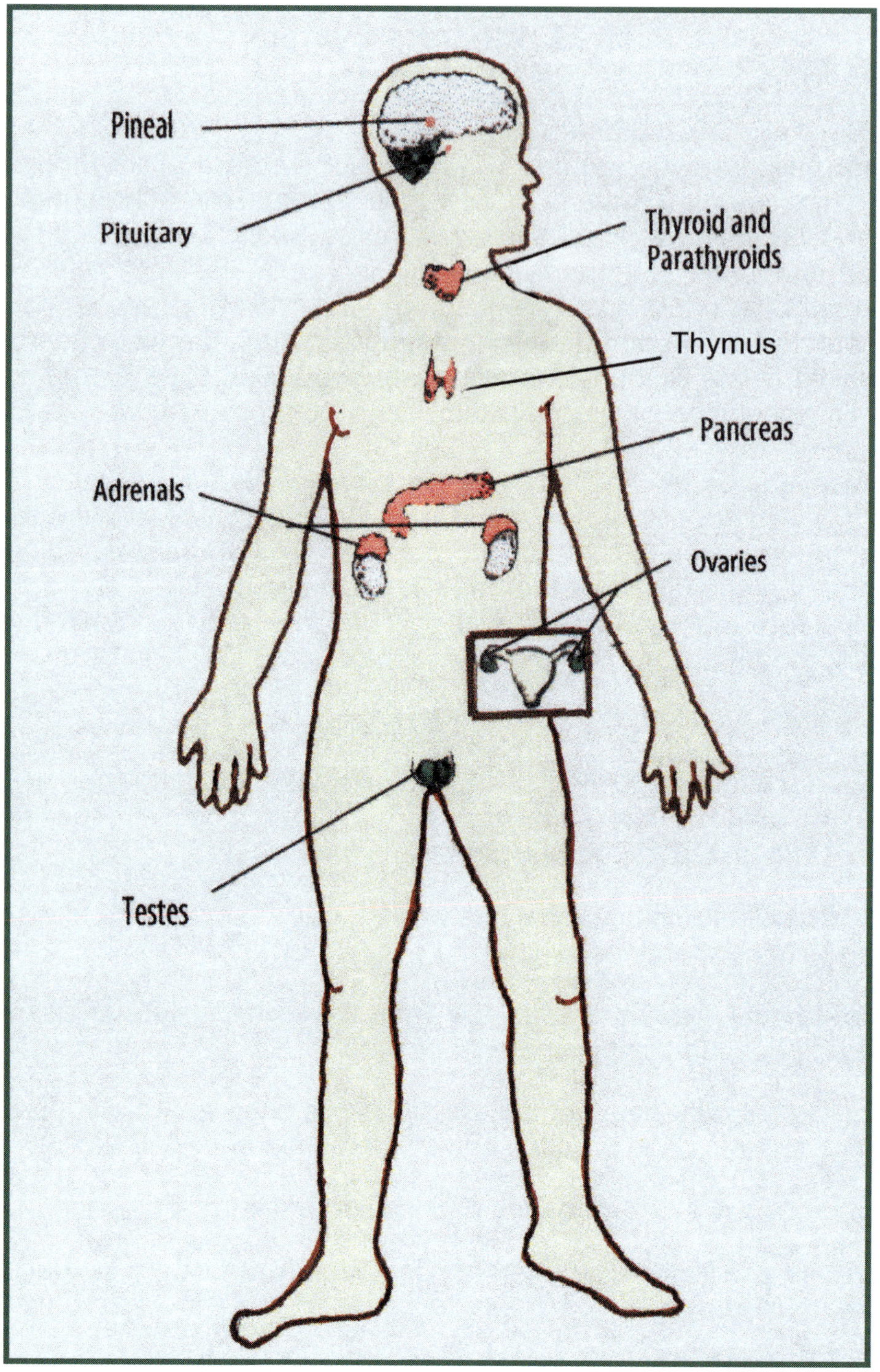

The Pineal, Pituitary, Thyroid, Parathyroids, Pancreas, Adrenals, Ovaries, Testes

THE ENDOCRINE SYSTEM: **The Fruit of the Spirit**

Hormones are to the physical body what the Fruit of the Spirit is to the spiritual body. The endocrine system consists of eight glands that produce and release hormones into the body to maintain homeostasis—the chemical balance—of its systems. The Spirit of God in believers produces nine traits, the fruit of the spirit, that are needed to maintain homeostasis, which is harmony and balance in the Body of Christ. When these traits are present they promote and enhance the activities of the Spirit of God in believers and those around them. Their absence hinders the activities of the Spirit.

The Fruit of the Spirit sets the tone for a prosperous life for the believer and a balanced environment in the church. "But the fruit of the Spirit is love, joy, peace, longsuffering, gentleness, goodness, faith, meekness, temperance: against such there is no law… If we live in the Spirit, let us also walk in the Spirit." (Galatians 5:22-23, 25) To walk in the Spirit means to live a life that is based on the principles of the Fruit of the Spirit.

The Pituitary Gland regulates many bodily activities from growth to reproduction. It is nicknamed the master gland. The pituitary is stimulated by the brain. **Love** is a type of spiritual hormone given by the master of creation, God. John, the beloved disciple, tells us, "Whoever does not love does not know God, because *God is love* . . . This is love: not that we loved God, but that he loved us and sent his Son as an atoning sacrifice for our sins. Dear friends, since God so loved us, we also ought to love one another… If anyone acknowledges that Jesus is the Son of God, God lives in him and he in God. And so we know and rely on the love God has for us. There is no fear in love. But perfect love drives out fear, because fear has to do with punishment." (I John 4:8,10,11,15,16,18 NIV)

Paul described to the church of Corinth how love permeates the very existence of relationships in the Body of Christ and is essential in personal growth and for the survival and growth of the church. "If I speak in the tongues of men and angels, if I have the gift of prophecy and know everything, if I have faith and give financial blessings to others, even if I sacrifice myself in flames for the cause of Christ, and I do not have love, I am nothing." (I Corinthians 13:1-3 paraphrased) Love is described as patient and kind, protecting, trusting, hopeful, perseveres and never fails. It is not envious, boastful, proud, rude, self-seeking, does not keep a record of wrongs or delight in evil. Of the traits faith, hope and love, love is the greatest. (I Corinthians 13:4-8 paraphrased)

The Thyroid Gland controls the rate of the body's metabolism, breaking down protein for energy or for tissue growth. **Joy** is the passion or emotion excited by the acquisition or expectation of good; pleasurable feelings or emotions caused by a sense of well-being. It is the emotional and spiritual level to which one returns after bursts of excitement or disappointment. It is a balanced homeostatic state of mind in which one lives day to day and is seen by others as enthusiasm or zest for life. Those who lack zest for life just survive, without pursuit of spiritual and/or emotional growth and development.

In the Old Testament, when Ezra and the priests taught the laws to the children of Israel and they began to understand, they were overjoyed and worshiped God, bowing and crying. Ezra told them to worship God and not to be sad or upset, because "the joy of the Lord is your strength." (Nehemiah 8:10b). Knowing and obeying God gives one a zest for living, a threshold of joy from which one may temporally deviate toward happiness or sadness, then return to a balanced, joyful state of mind. As the prophet Isaiah led the Israelites in thanksgiving for God's mercy, he expressed confidence in God's deliverance and zest for the present and future. "Behold, God is my salvation; I will trust, and not be afraid: for the Lord Jehovah is my strength and my song; he also is become my salvation. Therefore with joy shall ye draw water out of the wells of salvation." (Isaiah 12:2,3)

The Parathyroid Glands control the rate at which calcium is absorbed into the bones and phosphate is eliminated in urine. Calcium and phosphate are chemicals that have opposing functions, both of which are necessary for the body but must be kept in balance. In the spiritual sense, believers are advised to exhibit **temperance** in their daily lives, not extending themselves too far in either direction. The Bible advises temperance in pleasure, wine, oil, food, money and riches, work and in all walks of life. "He that loves pleasure will become poor; whoever loves wine and oil will never be rich." (Proverbs 21:17NIV) "Be ye angry, and sin not: let not the sun go down upon your wrath." (Ephesians 4:26) Temperance is defined as habitual moderation, self-control, abstinence.

The Adrenal Glands help control electrolyte balance, blood pressure, provide resistance to stress and produce anti-inflammatories. Hormones from the Adrenal Glands calm and keep the body free from disturbances that upset the homeostasis. **Peace** is a state of quiet or tranquility; freedom from disturbance or agitation; harmony or concord between individuals. A peaceful mind and spirit are the result of obedience to God and are another way in which there must be balance in the believer's life. They even have an effect on the physical body. The Psalmist said, "The Lord will give strength unto his people; the Lord will bless his people with peace." (Psalm 29:11) God told his people the Israelites that they would not have gotten into so much trouble and would not be so distraught had they followed his instructions, "O that thou hadst harkened to my commandments! then had thy peace been as a river." (Isaiah 48:18)

Christ, knowing he was about to leave this earth, left his disciples a legacy, "Peace I leave with you, my peace I give unto you: not as the world giveth, give I unto you. Let not your heart be troubled, neither let it be afraid." (John 14:27) In his farewell, Paul blessed the brethren of the church at Philippi, by saying, "And the peace of God, which passeth all understanding, shall keep your hearts and minds through Christ Jesus." (Philippians 4:7)

The Pancreas produces glucagons and insulin, which regulate blood sugar. While the hormone glucagon increases blood sugar, insulin is the hormone that helps to lower it. Either hormone in an uncontrolled state would result in physical death. **Meekness** is defined as mild of temper, not wild; tame, gentle, humble, not easily provoked. Although sons and daughters of God are capable of being aggressive, Jesus taught believers to be meek. When the soldiers came to arrest him, his disciple Peter pulled out his sword and cut off the ear of the high priest's servant. Jesus said to him, "Do you think I cannot call on my Father, and he will at once put at my disposal more than twelve legions of angels?" (Matthew 26:53 NIV) Instead, Jesus, in a spirit of meekness, humbled himself to suffer so that the Old Testament scriptures would be fulfilled and God's plan of salvation would be complete.

Jesus said, "Blessed are the meek: for they shall inherit the earth." (Matthew 5:5) The Psalmist said, "The meek shall eat and be satisfied: they shall praise the Lord that seek him: your heart shall live for ever." (Psalm 22:26)

On the other hand, at the proper time and for the principles of the gospel, Jesus was filled with righteous indignation and became aggressive. Using a whip he made of cords, he drove the people who were selling oxen and sheep and doves and the changers of money out of the temple. He overturned their tables and poured out their money. (John 2:13-16) Such people not only turned the temple into a market; they were dishonest in their dealings and took advantage of poor people.

The Ovaries and Testes secrete hormones that maintain the sexual characteristics of males and females. Testosterone is the male hormone that is responsible for the development of strongly defined male facial features, voice tone and quality, sex organs, development of musculature and bone growth. Estrogen is the female hormone that is responsible for development and ongoing maintenance of female curvatures and maintaining the ovarian cycle that is associated with reproduction. The sexual hormones give males and females strength and softness, roughness and kindness and general physical excellence.

Traits of gentleness and goodness are the finer qualities in believers, not to be mistaken for weakness. **Gentleness** is the act of being gentle; softness of manners, disposition, free of harshness or roughness. **Goodness** embraces excellence, strength; virtue, benevolence, kindness.

Paul told Timothy, "And the servant of the Lord must not strive (quarrel); but be gentle unto all men, apt (able) to teach, patient." (II Timothy 2:24) "But the wisdom that is from above is first pure, then peaceable, gentle, and easy to be entreated, full of mercy and good fruits, without partiality, and without hypocrisy." (James 3:17)

On the other hand, when God had a special job for the prophet Jeremiah to do and wanted him to confront and follow through with the people, he told him to, "be not afraid of their faces: for I am with thee to deliver thee. . . be not dismayed at their faces." (Jeremiah 1:8a, 17b) Both sexes have a role to play in their sexuality and are capable of kindness as well as firmness. Likewise, believers are capable of gentleness and goodness but when necessary, firm assertiveness.

The Pineal Gland inhibits ovarian function and is influenced by the light of day and darkness of night. This gland is located in the brain and keeps the ovaries from becoming active during childhood in females. It starts to degenerate at age seven and by adulthood, it is mostly fibrous tissue. **Longsuffering** is a trait we have all needed to receive of God and others. It means bearing injuries or provocation for a long time, patient, not easily provoked. During childhood and again as newborn believers, we need God's patience and for him to be slow to anger. However, as time goes on, with spiritual and emotional maturity, the need for God and people to be longsuffering on our behalf should diminish. Then it is our turn to show longsuffering toward others who are still maturing.

The church members were impatient at one time, because it seemed like people were getting away with their evil ways, going on as though Jesus had never come to change their lives. Peter reassured them, "The Lord is not slack concerning his promise, as some men count slackness; but is longsuffering to us-ward, not willing that any should perish, but that all should come to repentance." (II Peter 3:9) Paul gave a detailed description of love, and one of the ingredients was longsuffering. "Charity suffereth long, and is kind." (I Corinthians 13:4a) Jesus told his disciples, "Freely ye have received, freely give." (Matthew 10:8b) Believers must always be conscious of the fact that their lives would be much different had it not been for God's longsuffering on their behalf.

The Thymus is active in antibody production for defense of the body during infancy and childhood to approximately age seven. The body forms antibodies when it identifies a substance that could be harmful to the health of the individual. Once formed, they remain in the system and protect the body from a specific disease. **Faith** is a noun, the name of something. "It is the substance of things hoped for, the evidence of things not seen." (Hebrews 11:1) It originates in the spirit, and relates to the spiritual world. On the physical level, faith connects with the soul—the mind, in the form of belief, and is expressed by action on the part of the body. "Faith without works is dead." (James 2:20b)

Faith is involved in the initial process of salvation. "For by grace are ye saved through faith." (Ephesians 2:8a) It becomes the core of the believer's life and matures with his/her spiritual and emotional level. "For whatsoever is born of God overcometh the world: and this is the victory that overcometh the world, even our faith." (I John 5:4) "For, the just shall live by faith." (Galatians 3:11b) Paul wrote, "God has dealt to every man the *measure* of faith." (Romans 12:3b) Jesus said to his disciples, "If ye have faith as a grain of mustard seed, ye shall say unto this mountain, Remove hence to yonder place; and it shall remove; and nothing shall be impossible unto you." (Matthew 17:20b) Sometimes believers try to accelerate their level of faith through various spiritual exercises. But as a mustard seed grows, "Common faith" . . . similarly grows with experience over time (Titus 1:4) "For we walk by faith, not by sight" (II Corinthians 5:7) In this passage, Paul described a walk, a way of life centered in faith, belief and action.

The GIFT of faith usually accompanies a supernatural physical or emotional healing that is a mighty feat beyond the power of man. It is a special assurance of answered prayer before it happens (See Gifts of the Spirit, page 90).

Anger

Anger is a strong feeling of displeasure or hostility. It usually starts when we feel rejected or unloved, experience the loss of finance or a loved one and when we feel insecure, in danger or threatened. Anger poisons the system, having lingering physical and emotional effects. It can cause an increase in the blood pressure and pulse, change the tone of voice, interfere with digestion, breathing and circulation. Emotionally, anger causes depression and leads to passive-aggressive behaviors. Some people may eat excessively, go on elaborate shopping sprees or use alcohol or drugs due to suppressed anger.

There are varying degrees of anger:

Resentment refers to ill will and smoldering anger. It is a subtle, repressed, seething anger that can last for years. People are often afraid to express anger so they try to suppress (hide) it. Resentment is expressed in passive/aggressive behavior, and can explode on self and/or others, especially on innocent people.

Rage and fury apply to an intense, explosive, often destructive emotion. It is exhibited by aggressive behaviors directed toward people and circumstances.

Wrath applies to especially fervent anger that seeks vengeance or punishment.

Indignation is righteous anger at something wrongful, unjust or evil. It comes from love. Jesus acted in righteous indignation when he beat the money changers out of the temple. (Matthew 21:12&13)

WHEN ANGRY, AVOID:

- Making important decisions.
- Judging other people.
- Allowing anger to linger in your mind.

TO DEAL WITH PERSONAL ANGER:

- Recognize it and own up to it.
- Figure out what triggered the anger. Talk with someone if you need to.
- Deal with anger quickly. Satan will help you justify your angry feelings and will make it very hard to overcome them.
- Forgive.

Overcoming anger requires a change of attitude. Do not initiate close friendships with angry people. Some behaviors and attitudes are contagious, and situations that are dangerous to you could develop.[2]

---

[2] Notes from Television Lecture by Dr. Charles Stanley, (former president of the Southern Baptist Conference). In Touch" National Television Broadcast 2001

Forgiveness

To forgive is to grant pardon without harboring resentment. Based on the personal consequences of harboring resentment described in the preceding section, it is obvious that forgiveness is a gift to yourself. It is for *giving* to others, and as a result it sets you free.

To Forgive Another Individual

- Admit to yourself that you were wronged and identify the person who offended you.
- Experience and express the anger for a limited time period.
- Try to understand the circumstances from the offender's point of view.
- Put in perspective the actual harm you have experienced. You must remember what is most important to you. Are your salvation, your family and your life intact? What did you lose that God cannot restore?
- Think about the times that you hurt someone and needed to be forgiven. Thank God for forgiving you.
- Remember that if you do not forgive others, Christ will not forgive you.
- Offer forgiveness, even if the offender does not volunteer an apology.
- Ask God to help you to forgive fully and let it go.
- The Lord will not take it from you. You must give it to him, and then he will take it away. Refuse to allow the incident to replay in your mind. Let it go, cast it into the sea of forgetfulness where God has put your mistakes.
- Ask God also to heal the physical and emotional hurt associated with the incident. Believe that he has healed you, and be made whole.

Unforgiven people and situations that have festered in your mind long term will be difficult to let go. Once you begin to justify your position, you become hardened and feel you are right. Jesus told the Pharasee to forgive his brother seventy times seven (70X7=490) times a day. This means we must maintain an attitude of forgiveness in our way of life, so that we can easily and freely give it. As soon as we are wronged, forgive and let it go. The sooner you forgive the easier it will be, and It will become easier and easier as you practice it. Paul told the saints at Ephesus, "And be ye kind one to another, tenderhearted, forgiving one another, even as God for Christ's sake hath forgiven you." (Ephesians 4:32) Do now allow anyone to keep you in psychological bondage by your own anger. If you have sincerely followed the above steps and you still feel resentment, start over and do them again and again until the anger is gone.

You know you have fully forgiven an offender when you do not replay the incident in your mind every time you see him or her. Then, when the incident *does* come to mind the pain and anger that were associated with it are gone. Thank God for victory and be ready for the next time.

CHAPTER SUMMARY

SIMILARITIES BETWEEN THE ENDOCRINE SYSTEM AND THE FRUIT OF THE SPIRIT:

- The Endocrine System consists of glands that produce hormones to maintain the body's homeostasis. The Fruit of the Spirit maintains homeostasis, balance and harmony in the Body of Christ.

- The Endocrine Glands control vital life functions of the physical body such as growth, blood sugar level and reproduction. The elements of the Fruit of the Spirit are essential for the life and growth of the Body of Christ.

- These are the glands that produce hormones and nine Fruit of the Spirit:

    - The Pituitary gland compares to love, which permeates all relationships in the Body of Christ.
    - The Thyroid gland promotes a sense of wellbeing and hope, which is comparable to joy in the life of believers.
    - The Parathyroid glands are similar to temperance in that they are responsible for the balance of calcium and phosphorous.
    - The Adrenal glands calm the body, which is peace.
    - The Pancreas balances blood sugar and compares to meekness.
    - Ovaries and Testes produce male and female traits of gentleness and goodness.
    - The Pineal gland is active in childhood and goes away in adulthood. New believers need others to be longsuffering toward them at first and need it less as they mature and make fewer mistakes.
    - The Thymus gland produces many antibodies during childhood that stay in the body throughout our lives. Similarly, faith begins when we first believe and forms a foundation that stays with believers for life.

ANGER

- Starts when a person feels rejected or unloved, experiences loss or insecurity.
- Anger that goes unchecked festers into resentment and affects behaviors.
- We must recognize and own up to anger and forgive.

FORGIVENESS

- To forgive is to grant pardon without harboring resentment.
- Forgiveness is more beneficial to oneself than to anyone else.

CHAPTER ELEVEN
The Respiratory System

The cells of the physical body need a continuous supply of oxygen to carry out the activities that are vital to their survival. Oxygen is the gas that blood carries to the cells, and carbon dioxide is the gas that blood carries from the cells. The respiratory system maintains blood gas balance—homeostasis—by the exchange of oxygen and carbon dioxide. Respiration is the process of taking in oxygen and letting go of carbon dioxide. An excessive amount of carbon dioxide is poisonous to cells and must be quickly and efficiently eliminated.

The organs that make up the respiratory system are the nose, pharynx, larynx, trachea, bronchi and lungs.

The respiratory and circulatory systems participate equally in respiration. Failure of either the circulatory system to circulate blood or the respiratory system to exchange oxygen and carbon dioxide results in rapid death of cells from oxygen starvation and disruption of the body's homeostasis.

Three basic processes of respiration are:

- **Ventilation** is breathing—the movement of air between the atmosphere and lungs.
- **Inspiration** is breathing in—the muscle between the lungs and abdominal cavity (diaphragm) moves downward and the ribs move up and outward. Muscles of the chest wall contract, increasing the space in the chest cavity, causing air to flow into the lungs. This involves total intake of atmospheric gases and particles. Larger particles are caught in the hairs of the nostrils.
- **Expiration** is breathing out—the muscles relax, decreasing the space in the chest cavity; then air flows out of the lungs.

Two types of respiration are:

- **External respiration** is the exchange of oxygen between the lungs and blood.
- **Internal respiration** is the exchange of oxygen between blood and the cells.

When the level of hemoglobin in the blood is low, the amount of oxygen that is available to the cells is reduced. For cells to get the amount of oxygen they need, the body increases the rate of respiration and the heart rate. [1]

---

[1] Gerard J. Tortora and Nicholas Anagnostakos, Principles of Anatomy and Physiology (San Francisco: Canfield Press, 1975), pp. 429-448

THE RESPIRATORY SYSTEM

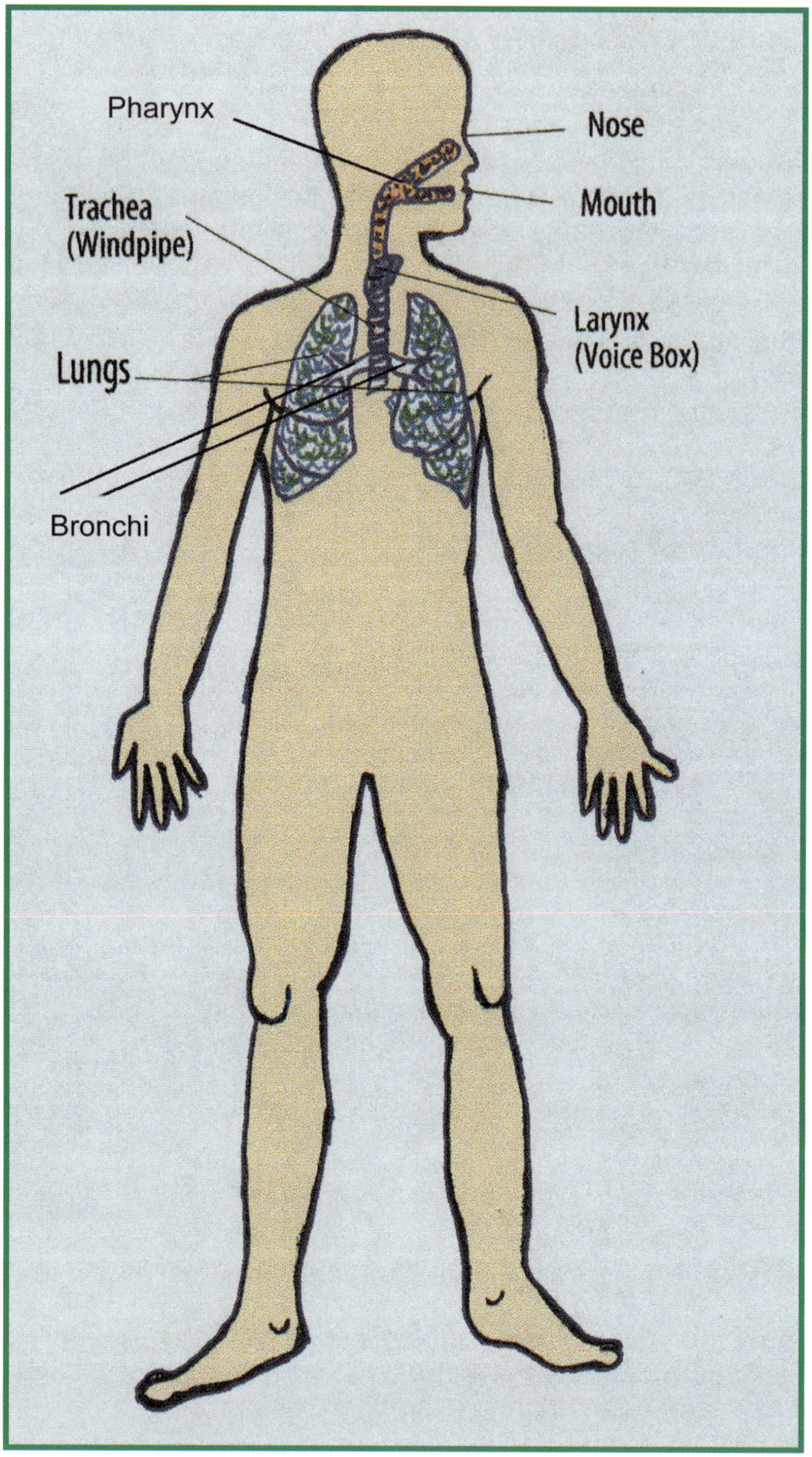

Nose, Pharynx, Larynx, Trachea, Bronchi, Lungs

<u>THE RESPIRATORY SYSTEM: **Prayer and Belief**</u>

While the process of taking in oxygen and letting go of carbon dioxide is called physical respiration, spiritual respiration is the process of satisfying needs by believing and letting go of "cares" through prayer, resulting in a renewed mind and spirit. Blood plays an integral part in the process of respiration, as carrier of the nutrients, oxygen and carbon dioxide. In the spiritual body, the Word of God is the carrier of nutrients for believers. It identifies the cares that hold us down and the weights we need to let go. The Word of God also contains vital promises that if we believe will sustain our strength and provide for growth of the spirit and soul.

In the course of a day spent going to work, dealing with family issues and the fulfilling of their ministries, believers accumulate "cares." Cares may be burdens carried for others, finances, hurt feelings, anger, disappointment, anxieties, pain, sadness and other weights that cloud our focus on spiritual goals or weaken our lines of communication with God. These cares are comparable to carbon dioxide in the cells, a waste product that is produced when cells perform their normal daily functions. As the build-up of carbon dioxide is poisonous to cells, a build up of cares is harmful to believers and in both instances the build-up must be eliminated to sustain spiritual, emotional and physical life.

<u>*Physical ventilation is breathing, movement of air between the atmosphere and lungs.*</u> Spiritual ventilation is receiving the refreshing and renewal of the spirit from the Word and in exchange, releasing the cares and weights of this world through prayer. Paul said, "But though our outward man perish, yet the inward man is renewed day by day." (II Corinthians 4:16b) After a long day of teaching and feeding the multitude of people, Jesus needed to ventilate. "And when he had sent the multitudes away, he went up into a mountain apart to pray: and when the evening was come, he was there alone." (Matthew 14:23)

<u>*Expiration is breathing OUT. Muscles of the chest wall relax, decreasing the space in the chest cavity, and air flows out of the lungs.*</u> Prayer is a time to relax and bare the soul before God, who knows us better than we know ourselves. When approaching the Lord in prayer, one must give him the cares that weigh on the mind and express a desire to overcome sins that cause the mind and spirit to live in bondage. "Let us lay aside every weight, and the sin which doth so easily beset us." (Hebrews 12:1b)

The scriptures advise us to:

- "Pray without ceasing." (I Thessalonians 5:17)
- "Be careful for nothing; but in everything by prayer and supplication with thanksgiving let your requests be made known unto God." (Philippians 4:6)
- "Casting all your care upon him; for he careth for you." (I Peter 5:7)
- "For we have not an high priest which cannot be touched with the feeling of our infirmities; but was in all points tempted like as we are, yet without sin. Let us therefore come boldly unto the throne of grace, that we may obtain mercy, and find grace to help in time of need." (Hebrews 4:15-16)
- Jesus said to his disciples, "Therefore I say unto you, What things soever ye desire, when ye pray, believe that ye receive them, and ye shall have them. And

when ye stand praying, forgive, if ye have ought against any: that your Father also which is in heaven may forgive you your trespasses." (Mark 11:24-25)

The purging process of prayer should leave the spirit void of cares and ready for a new start, as the chest feels after a slow, forceful expiration through pursed lips, blowing all of the air out of the lungs. The next step is automatic—*inhale!* The motion picture "*Waiting to Exhale,*[2]" portrays continuous upheavals in the lives of several single females as they live in anticipation of a time when they can relax, rid themselves of their problems and pasts, exhale and begin again.

Jesus' disciples asked him to teach them to pray, and his example (Matthew 6:9-13) has been labeled the Lord's Prayer. Some of the elements of prayer that could involve one or several prayers are:

- Acknowledge God as the Father.
- Worship him for who He is, Praise him for what He has done.
- Acknowledge his kingdom in heaven and on earth, submit to his will.
- Pray for our country and all levels of leadership.
- Ask for needs: personal, financial, worries, cares and others.
- Ask for God's forgiveness and acknowledge forgiveness given to others.
- Request assistance and strength in overcoming evil and temptations that cloud your vision or stunt spiritual, emotional or physical growth or health.
- Acknowledge again God's eternal kingship, his infinite power and abilities and give him thanks and glory for what he has done and will do.
- Ask these things in Jesus' name, Amen.

Inspiration is breathing IN. The chest cavity expands, making room for air by moving the ribs up and outward and the diaphragm down. Then air flows in, with all the gases and particles from the atmosphere. After baring the soul to God, one must open spirit and soul to God's Word, expecting to receive God's refreshing and renewing. The Psalmist wrote, "Hear my cry, O God; attend unto my prayer. From the end of the earth will I cry unto thee, when my heart is overwhelmed: lead me to the rock that is higher than I. For thou has been a shelter for me, and a strong tower from the enemy… I will trust in the covert of thy wings … So will I sing praise unto thy name for ever, that I may daily perform my vows." (Psalm 61:1-3, 4b,8) From his own broken spirit, David reached out for the Lord. Then his confidence and trust in the Lord were strengthened as he remembered past experiences of God's goodness. David ends the passage with renewed confidence and commitment. He was *singing* with an uplifted spirit and body. Note the progression of communication, spirit to soul to body. Sometime the spirit may be so broken that the soul-mind has to take the first step toward God, reaching up out of obedience or desperation, and soon the spirit follows. The beautiful thing about prayer is that at any time and in any place we can exhale our cares through prayer, then inhale, taking in a dose of God's promises from His Word, resulting in a refreshing of the spirit, soul and body.

---

[2] Executive Producer/Screenplay Terry McMillan; Producers Ezra Swerdlow, Deborah Schindler; Director Forest Waiting to Exhale (Whitaker Twentieth Century Fox, 1996)

Internal respiration takes place when oxygen is absorbed into the cells from the blood. Considering that oxygen is a need, getting it into the nose, airway and lungs is not enough. Oxygen must be absorbed into the blood and then into the cells to sustain life. To receive from God, one must "believe that he is, and that he is a rewarder of them that diligently seek him." (Hebrews 11:6b) "For the word of God is quick and powerful, and sharper than any twoedged sword, piercing even to the dividing asunder of soul and spirit, and of the joints and marrow, and is a discerner of the thoughts and intents of the heart." (Hebrews 4:12) So make an honest assessment of your needs, shortcomings, fears, aspirations and goals; then receive them from God by internalizing, digesting and believing the scriptures. Belief stimulates action. Those who take action know that results follow. David said, "This poor man cried, and the Lord heard him and saved him out of all his troubles." (Psalm 34:6) The scriptures show that David, a warrior, was a man of action.

Belief is about having confidence in the Word, God and one's self. The Hebrew church was told, "Cast not away therefore your confidence, which hath great recompence of reward. For ye have need of patience, that, after ye have done the will of God, ye might receive the promise." (Hebrews 10:35,36) Belief also requires patience and involves obedience to the will of God. Recompense means amends made for loss; it is compensation, payment for a service.

When the cells receive oxygen, they use it to carry out their purpose—reproducing, fighting disease, growing and so on. Belief is the element of the soul that causes one to carry out, follow through on life's purpose. "Faith, by itself, if it is not accompanied by action, is dead." (James 2:17bNIV) *Belief in the soul grows along with faith in the spirit.* It starts with salvation. "For God so loved the world, that he gave his only begotten Son, that whosoever believeth in him should not perish, but have everlasting life." (John 3:16) Then belief increases to meet the challenges of life. A man came to Jesus asking that his son be healed of a "dumb spirit." "Jesus said unto him, If thou canst believe, all things are possible to him that believeth. And straightway the father of the child cried out, and said with tears, Lord, I believe, help thou mine unbelief." (Mark 9:23,24) What an appropriate response for one who wanted so much for his son to be healed but knew that he could not imagine how it would materialize. In his spirit, he knew he had faith that Jesus could heal because he had seen it in others. When Jesus said he had to believe, the man quickly and properly assessed his level of belief, gave all he had and asked the Lord to supply what was lacking. "Help thou my unbelief."

The fact that God's divine ability surpasses what we can ask or think tells us that in order to experience the fullness of his goodness, there are times when we must say to God, "Lord I believe, help thou my unbelief" to experience the next level of God's power. Paul said to the church at Ephesus, "Now unto him that is able to do exceeding abundantly above all that we ask or think, according to the power that worketh in us." (Ephesians 3:20) The suffix 'eth' means ongoing or continuously. "He that believ*eth*," therefore, continues to believe and keeps the connection intact. In return, the power work*eth* in us. On their wedding day, a couple believes they were made for each other. For the marriage to last, the couple *believeth* in each other and therefore has the power to weather the storms of life and grow old together. Continuous belief in spite of disappointments, pain and mistakes results in victory because one is willing and consistent in working through the obstacles.

When the level of hemoglobin in the blood is low, the amount of oxygen that is available to the cells is low. The medical term applied to this is anemia. Hemoglobin is the agent in blood that attaches to oxygen to carry it to the cells. Spiritually, when the Word of God is lacking in a believer's life or when the Word he/she receives from external sources is of insufficient quality, the believer's options for receiving from God are limited. They find themselves running from church to church and in and out of different faiths, searching for a need they cannot identify, or they just stay where they are, too weak to search for knowledge. Believers are responsible to themselves and God to find a church home where they are taught to grow to spiritual maturity and fulfill their spiritual purpose in the world. "How shall they believe in him of whom they have not heard?" (Romans 10:14b)

THE RESPIRATORY SYSTEM ■ PATHOLOGY
Negative Attitude & Unbelief

Attitudes may be regarded as an individual's state of mental readiness or unspoken outlook on life, which consistently controls his or her responses to many aspects of life. These responses are usually directed toward some object, person or group. Although attitudes are seen as enduring, they are learned responses rather than genetic. Therefore, we have the power to change them.

Attitude refers to a state of mind or a feeling. A negative attitude limits our lives, causing us to be unforgiving, rigid, distrustful and unable to overcome or start over. When we have a negative attitude, we create situations in which we become frustrated, powerless and ill equipped to find solutions. "Awfulizing" is a concept that means we have learned to take whatever happens to us and say to ourselves, "Ain't it awful!" Sometimes it feels good to be downright negative, but most of the time, it only makes us feel worse. Things happen, and we are the ones that make them positive or negative experiences.[3]

Living in a negative world takes a toll on the physical body. Constant distrust and suspicions generate tension, resulting in stress and all of the medical conditions that accompany it—hypertension, increased heart rate, insomnia, obesity etc. The ability to change our lives becomes more and more difficult when we have no positive thoughts and perceive that there are no options that we can trust to help us overcome. Remember, however, we *can* control and change our attitude.

A long-term negative attitude leads to unbelief. While belief propels us toward a goal or an outcome, unbelief is paralyzing. One who does not believe in himself, in God or His Son, will not act on the divine promises. Jesus did not perform many mighty works for the people in his home town, the city of Jerusalem, because of their unbelief. (Matthew 13:58) If Jesus was unable to overturn outcomes due to the power of people's unbelief, how much greater an obstacle it is for us.

Overcoming unbelief starts with a personal attitude adjustment that begins by taking an honest look into our hearts—the mind and all that motivates it. Mentally exhale and make a conscious decision to let go of all of the negative thoughts and feelings that bind your spirit, while physically blowing air through puckered lips. Then, reaching toward a higher calling, mentally inhale while taking in a very deep breath and take on all the strength and goodness you need. Paul told the Philippians, "Forgetting those things

---

[3] Philip Zimbardo & Ebbe Ebbesen Influencing Attitudes and Changing Behavior (Reading: Addison-Wesley Publishing Co., 1969), pp. 6-8

which are behind, and reaching forth unto those things which are before, I press toward the mark for the prize of the of the high calling of God in Christ Jesus." (Philippians 3:13) The writer told the Hebrews, "Let us lay aside every weight, and the sin which doth so easily beset us, and let us run with patience the race that is set before us, looking unto Jesus the author and finisher of our faith;" (Hebrews 12:1b-2a). Practice this exercise over and over, letting go of negativity a tiny bit at a time and replacing it little by little with strength and courage from the Word. Healthy individuals breathe at a rate of 16-20 times a minute. This allows us many opportunities to *let go* and *take on,* a constant refreshing and renewal of the spirit and soul!

THE RESPIRATORY SYSTEM ♥ HEALTH & WELLNESS
Humor/Laughter

Juggling the demands of job and family while dealing with the many stresses, uncertainties, opportunities and changes of life can leave us feeling drained and joyless. To face these sometimes overwhelming challenges, we must develop and cherish opportunities for humor. Humor is the ability to see and *tastefully* express what is funny, ludicrous and amusing in the course of life. Through humor we establish relationships, relieve tension, release anger, facilitate learning and cope more effectively with all kinds of pain. It allows us to laugh. Laughter improves our productivity without hindering our concentration. It energizes us and eases the stress and boredom of repetitive tasks. Laughter is the antidote for the stress that causes illness, depression, insomnia, burnout and absenteeism from our jobs. Fun and laughter stimulate creativity and innovation in our lives.

Our bodies benefit from laughter because laughing makes us take deeper breaths than usual, filling our lungs with a surplus of oxygen. This excess oxygen is absorbed into the blood cells in the lungs and travels to the heart, where it is pumped through large and small arteries to the brain and all body cells. The result is a welcome refreshing of the cells, causing a strengthening of the heart muscle, a boost to the immune system to fight off illness and a release of endorphins—the body's natural pain killers—that actually diminish the body's physical and psychological perception of pain. Sustained laughter utilizes the abdominal, facial and skeletal muscles, the joints, nerves and circulatory system. It even helps some people lower their blood pressure. I read once that laughter is like jogging on the inside, and that one hundred chuckles a day is equal to ten minutes of rowing.

Our humor and laughter can help us cope, recover and heal. They allow us to detach from the current situation for a few minutes and feel respite from the emotional chaos that sometimes surrounds us. Feelings of anger, tension and fear can be neutralized and released with laughter. After laughing, we feel strong, resilient and hopeful. Laughter invites celebration and reminds us of the joy of life. In the midst of tragic circumstances, it sets the spirit free, allowing us a chance to clear our heads and restore our sense of balance.[4] Humor is integral to our peace of mind and our ability to go beyond survival. Solomon said, "A cheerful heart is good medicine, but a crushed spirit dries up the bones." (Proverbs 17:22NIV)

---

[4] Nursing Profile Humor's A Step Toward Healing After Terrorist Attacks (Patty Wooten & Ed Dunkelblau,December, 2001), pp. 14,15

CHAPTER SUMMARY

SIMILARITIES BETWEEN THE RESPIRATORY SYSTEM AND THE REFRESHING OF PRAYER AND BELIEF:

- The respiratory system maintains blood-gas homeostasis in the physical body while prayer and belief maintain homeostasis, balance in the spiritual life of believers.
- The accumulation of carbon dioxide in the cells is as detrimental to the life of cells as an accumulation of cares is to the spiritual life of believers.
- Respiration is taking in oxygen and letting go of carbon dioxide. Spiritual respiration is taking in the promises of God and letting go of cares, resulting in the renewal of the spirit and soul.
- Ventilation is inspiration and expiration; spiritual ventilation is praying and believing, resulting in a renewing of the mind and spirit.
- Expiration is breathing out carbon dioxide. Prayer is giving up to God the cares and weights that block spiritual growth.
- Inspiration is taking in oxygen. Spiritual inspiration is taking in the refreshing promises of the Word of God—being renewed by His grace and enlightened by His light.
- Internal spiritual respiration takes place when God's promise is fulfilled in thought, word and deed.
- Believers are responsible to find a church home where they are taught to grow to spiritual maturity and fulfill their spiritual purpose in the world.

NEGATIVE ATTITUDE & UNBELIEF, HUMOR & LAUGHTER

- Attitudes are learned responses rather than genetic; therefore, we can change our own attitude.
- A negative attitude leads to unbelief. Belief propels us toward a goal or an outcome. Unbelief is paralyzing.
- Humor is the ability to see and tastefully express what is funny, ludicrous and amusing in the course of life. Laughter greatly involves the respiratory system and has positive effects for the total body.

CHAPTER TWELVE
The Urinary System

The metabolism (breakdown) of food in the body results in the production of waste by the cells, including carbon dioxide and excess water and heat. Protein breakdown produces the toxic chemicals ammonia and urea. Excess amounts of essential ions such as sodium, chloride, sulfate, phosphate and hydrogen accumulate in the body. These toxic materials, the excess fluid and excess essential ions must be eliminated from the body.

The primary function of the urinary system is to keep the body in homeostasis by controlling the concentration of and volume of fluid in the body and remove waste. This is accomplished through a filtering (straining) process performed by the kidneys, which manufacture urine as the end product. The urinary system is comprised of two kidneys, two ureters, one urinary bladder and a single urethra. The kidneys perform the major work of the urinary system through three functions that produce urine: filtration, reabsorption and excretion. Normal kidneys filter out of the body system one to two ounces of urine waste per hour, depending on the level of an individual's fluid intake.

- **Filtration** – Is the forcing of fluids and dissolved substances through a membrane by an outside pressure. Filtration occurs when blood enters the tiny tubes in the kidneys and the body's blood pressure forces the excess water and waste components through microscopic holes in the walls of the tubes. The filtered solution (filtrate) consists of sodium, potassium, chloride, sulfate, glucose, ammonia, urea, creatinine and protein.
- **Reabsorption** – The movement of the filtered solution back into the blood is reabsorption. This is a very discriminating process, because only specific amounts of specific substances are reabsorbed, depending on the needs of the body at a particular moment. Reabsorption is carried out through both passive and active mechanisms of transport.
- **Excretion** – After needed ions have been reabsorbed, excretion is the process during which adjustments are made in the acid level (pH) of the remaining filtered solution in the kidneys, and the body eliminates the solution as waste.

THE EFFECTS OF HYPERTENSION ON THE KIDNEYS

The kidneys are damaged when there is prolonged hypertension because the excessive pressure on the tiny holes in the tubes of the kidneys causes them to stretch and lose their ability to properly strain the blood. This interferes with the kidney's ability to filtrate and reabsorb sodium, potassium, chloride, sulfate, ammonia, glucose, urea, creatinine and protein. Then there is a loss of homeostasis or balance in the internal environment of the body. Without intervention, the outcome is death.[1]

---

[1] Gerard J. Tortora and Nicholas Anagnostakos, Principles of Anatomy and Physiology (San Francisco: Canfield Press, 1975), pp. 511-529

THE URINARY SYSTEM

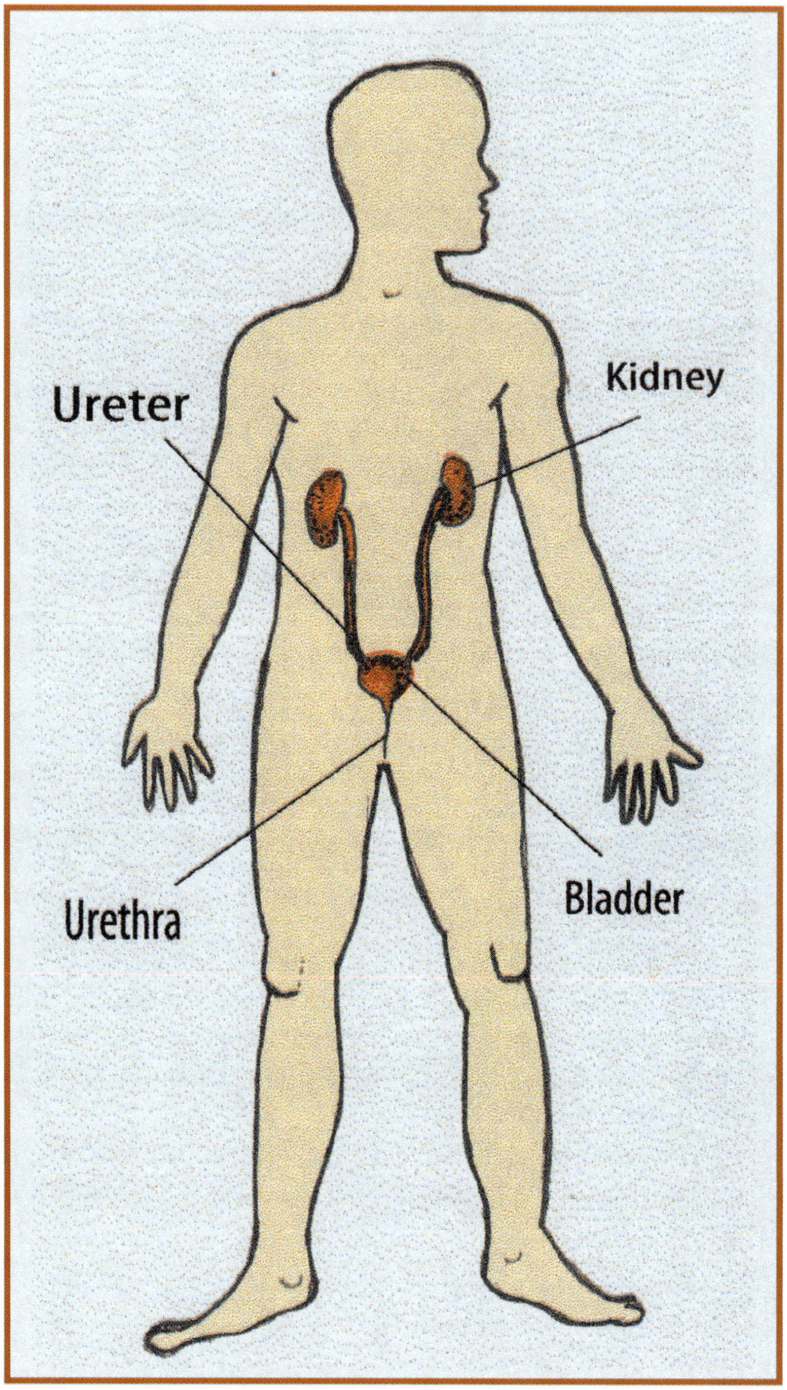

Kidneys, Ureters, Bladder and Urethra

THE URINARY SYSTEM: **Commit to the Cause**

In the course of our day-to-day lives, psychological and spiritual waste accumulates in the form of cares, an excess of essentially good traits and wasted time. Individuals having a desire to grow personally and spiritually, while contributing to society and the Body of Christ, must build into their way of life a process whereby such wastes can be eliminated from their lives. Waste (described as "cares" in Chapter Eleven) include burdens, anger, anxieties, pain, hurt feelings, disappointment, sadness, financial worries etc. "Cares" are toxic feelings that can develop into more serious emotions that are harmful to our physical health. They do not belong in anyone's life for extended periods of time and must be eliminated. Essential traits such as love, gentleness, goodness, meekness, longsuffering and other gracious traits (the Fruit of the Spirit), when allowed to be misused by others, tend to spawn psychological and spiritual toxins. Unmanaged, wasted time results from a lack of focus and interferes with one's ability to fully commit to a cause.

Many people read and do not comprehend, listen and do not hear, perform and do not accomplish. Their desire is real, and the cause is substantial, but there is little measurable gain on any front. Paul described this trend among the members of the church in Rome. "For I bear them record that they have a zeal of God, but not according to knowledge. For they being ignorant of God's righteousness, and going about to establish their own righteousness, have not submitted themselves unto the righteousness of God." (Romans 10:2-3) The trend is universal; people are busy, going to and fro, stressed out. What is the purpose, and what is being accomplished?

This last chapter, requiring your thoughtful scrutiny and participation, will guide you through some steps that will help you sort through your life, make decisions and set priorities that will enhance your spirit, soul and body. What is your purpose? What are you accomplishing in life? It is the writer's intent that some thoughts along these lines have been developing in your mind while reading the preceding chapters and that you now have:

- A clear vision of your level of spiritual maturity and your potential to be a contributing, functional cell in the Body of Christ,
- An uplifted spirit that connects with God's spirit,
- An enriched soul that draws from the spirit and enhances the body,
- A goal to care for and optimize the health of the physical body God gave you.

Readers should now study to gain more knowledge in the subjects that were briefly introduced and respond with a commitment to the cause or causes to which you feel drawn. Your "cause" may be for spiritual or emotional growth, for your health or a project. It will require a plan and expectations for the results. You must have a passion and feel the urgency to realize this goal. In the medical field, a sense of *urgency* is what one feels 30-45 minutes after consuming a super sized drink from a favorite fast-food vendor. Without a doubt it's going to happen, maybe not immediately, but it will. So plan for where, be ready for when and assemble all the necessary equipment, because *it will happen*.

Jesus, talking to the multitude about becoming his disciples, said, "For which of you, intending to build a tower, sitteth not down first, and counteth the cost, whether he have sufficient to finish it?" (Luke 14:28) Building a tower is a long-term commitment, and there are many things to consider before starting the project: time, money, manpower, architectural design, city building codes, contractors and so on. Making a commitment to a cause whether spiritual, emotional, physical or financial requires imagining a desired outcome, thinking through how to get there and planning the stages. There are decisions to be made concerning time and money management, personal sacrifice, logistics and feasibility. Successful plans require that we remain focused and practice assertiveness.

The kidneys perform three functions that can be applied to the way we live: filtration, reabsorption and excretion.

<u>*Filtration involves the forcing of fluids through a membrane by an outside pressure.*</u> When blood passes through the fine mesh membranes of the tubes in the kidneys a solution called filtrate is left. It is like the residue that remains in the strainer when liquid containing particles is poured through. The following exercise is a simplified means of evaluating the level of homeostasis-balance in your personal life. It will help you determine whether your way of life supports what you believe and what is most valuable to you.

ON A SHEET OF PAPER

- **List your beliefs** –

Example:

  - 1. God should be the center of my life.
  - 2. It is my responsibility to keep my body healthy to the extent that it is physically possible.
  - 3. I believe that I can contribute to the business success of my employer

- **List your values** - what is most important in your life, your philosophy.
  Example:
  1. Family comes first, then job or friends.
  2. Education is important.
  3. Exercise, tithing and/or fun are important to me.
  4. My job provides the means for me to support myself and my family.

ON ANOTHER PAGE, DRAW TWO VERTICAL LINES TO CREATE THREE COLUMNS *OR* <u>MAKE SEVERAL COPIES OF PAGE 123</u>

- **Column 1: List ALL of your activities during the last month.**
  Example: Work, swim, church, TV, school, study etc.
  Put one activity on each horizontal line.

- **Column 2: By each activity, write the total amount of time you spent on it in hours during the month.** (One hour per week = 4 hours per month)

COLUMN 1 – Activities	COLUMN 2 - Time	COLUMN 3 – Belief/Value
Swimming	4 Hours	
Church	5 Hours	
Work	160 Hours	
Television	200 Hours	

<u>Table 4</u> Written Exercise

By listing your activities and associating the amount of time spent on them you can see your "way of life" in front of you, on paper. Our kidneys do something like this as all of our blood circulates through them. On a regular basis, they "look" at the content of the blood and the amount of the chemicals and gases that it contains. This tells the kidneys how the total body is doing.

- **Cover the column of activities and make a mental note of time periods that are extremely long and those that are short.**

You have now identified blocks of time that need further consideration. The activities associated with these blocks of time are like the substance left in the strainer when you pour a solution through it. They require evaluation and thought, so they go on to the next stage, reabsorption. The chemicals and fluid left in the strainer are the *filtrate*. The kidneys then reconsider these filtered chemicals in a process called reabsorption.

<u>Reabsorption is moving specific amounts of necessary substances back into the blood, depending on the needs of the body at a particular moment.</u> In the kidneys the chemical balance of the body is assessed and the needed amount of each chemical is reabsorbed from the filtrate back into the blood. This means the kidneys check the level of each chemical and ion and the level of fluid and acid in the system to determine the body's need for each one. Only the specific chemical and the amount of the chemical or fluid necessary to sustain life are *reabsorbed* back into the blood.

RETURN TO THE WRITTEN EXERCISE:

- **Write the belief or value that each activity supports in Column #3**. If the activity does not match a belief or value, write NAV meaning Non-Added-Value.

COLUMN 1 – Activities	COLUMN 2 - Time	COLUMN 3 – Belief/Value
Swimming	4 Hours	Healthy Body
Church	5 Hours	God Is the Leader of my Life
Work	160 Hours	Support self and family
Television	200 Hours	NAV

<u>Table 5</u> Written Exercise

- **Put a check by the activities that support your beliefs and values but should be done more or less.**

- **Adjust the time column to the amount of time that *should* be spent on the activity.**
- **Write in activities, beliefs and values that should be added to your life to sustain your spirit, soul and body. Match a belief or value to each additional activity.**

Review the list, taking your time to make adjustments where needed, for beliefs, values and activities. This is the new pattern for your balanced life. You may want to rewrite the final list on a new sheet. These are the activities that you have determined are necessary to support balance in your life and sustain the health of your spirit, soul and body. Reabsorption takes place when you make adjustments in your way of life utilizing your new plan. *Do these activities.*

Excretion is the process in which adjustments are made to the pH—acid content--of the body and the body gets rid of its waste. Once the kidneys determine that the body does not need the chemicals and fluids in the filtrate, they are eliminated from the body as urine.

- **Circle the non-value added activities, those that neither enhance nor improve your life, nor support your beliefs and values**.

These activities are the scum left in the strainer and *must be eliminated.* While some activities may be eliminated passively, through confession and making minor changes in past practices, others must be actively eliminated by seeking help, such as smoking cessation classes, marriage counseling or substance abuse classes etc. Whatever it takes, you must take the time and make the change to be successful.

This is the point at which adjustments are made by the choices you make to accommodate the new goals and eliminate wasteful cares, excess essential traits and unmanaged time. This process of change requires assertiveness with friends, family and self, but the results will be measurable and rewarding.

The kidneys go through this process every minute of the day. But individuals having goals whether large or small should utilize the above process to filter, reabsorb and excrete every six months or more frequently, based on your particular mission.

GETTING STARTED

There are people who have a desire or dream to do special things but do not because they are waiting for a sign from God. Others fail to act on their convictions until they are overtaken by an illness or have a close call with death. Why wait for adversity? A person dedicated to the Lord and living a life that honors Him has a daily intimacy with God. Through the Word, he/she knows what pleases Him and is capable of designing a plan under divine guidance, in which case there is no need for a sign. A plan that does not violate the Ten Commandments or principles of the Sermon on the Mount, or any other known scripture and is honorable is worth starting. A detailed plan includes tiny steps with realistic time lines. While working your plan, remain tuned in to God's Spirit and walk by faith to receive guidance. It is easier to guide a mind in motion than it is to start one that is motionless. Remember, Jesus selected his disciples from individuals he saw *working,* and the scriptures encourage working. "Let him that stole steal no more: but rather let him labour, working with his hands the thing which is good, that he may have to give to him that needeth." (Ephesians 4:28) Furthermore, the Psalmist said, "The steps of a good man are ordered by the Lord: and he delighteth in his way." (Psalm 37:23) Strive to be like David, of whom God gave testimony and said, "I have found David the son of Jesse, a man after mine own heart, which shall fulfill all my will." (Acts 13:22b) What an honor that God would have such confidence in a man!!

BELIEFS, VALUES AND PRIORITIES

One might ask, what determines beliefs, values and priorities? The Old Testament prophet Amos wrote a quotation from God to the Israelites, in which God talked about standing on a wall and setting a plumbline in the middle of the people that would be a standard of measurement for their lives (Amos 7:7,8). The plumbline today is Jesus, who lived on the earth and set a standard for our lives that is recorded in God's Word. It is internal, the Holy Spirit that holds us to the *higher* standard. The apostle Paul told Timothy, "The Spirit clearly says that in later times some will abandon the faith and follow deceiving spirits and things taught by demons. . . Train yourself to be godly. For physical training is of some value, but godliness has value for all things, holding promise for both the present life and the life to come. . . Don't let anyone look down on you because you are young, but set an example for the believers in speech, in life, in love, in faith and in purity." (I Timothy 4:1, 7b, 8,12NIV)

THE URINARY SYSTEM ■ PATHOLOGY

Stress

Our lives become more complicated as we mature, and expectations on the job and at home add responsibilities and tasks to our daily routine. We find ourselves running here and there for multiple causes and pursuits, striving to fulfill our own expectations and the real and/or perceived expectations of others. Then when physical signs of wear and tear begin to develop in our bodies, we just add a doctor's appointment to our busy schedules and continue our frantic way of life. Many of us would rather continue a way of life that is detrimental to our health and wait to be hospitalized than take time out to work through the life-planning process outlined in the previous section.

We are responsible to ourselves, our families and to God to effectively manage our lives so that we are productive in all areas. The honest opinion of a friend would probably reveal that some of our many tasks or responsibilities are not performed as effectively as we imagine due to a lack of time to plan, organize and prioritize. Overcommitted time is a result of having no focus or one that is too broad or general for too long, resulting in stress. There are two types of stressors—positive stressors motivate one to achieve, while negative stressors can push one beyond physical and emotional limits.

Persons undergoing severe negative stress feel helpless, hopeless and defeated. Stress is a mentally or emotionally disruptive or upsetting condition occurring in response to adverse external influences and is usually characterized by increased heart rate, high blood pressure, muscular tension and irritability. It decreases the effectiveness of the immune system, leading to an increased potential for musculoskeletal strains and sprains, infections, cancer and psychological depression. Stress increases blood levels of homocysteine, a chemical tied to heart disease and heart attack deaths. High levels of this amino acid are thought to injure the inside walls of blood vessels, promoting clots and blocking arteries that cause heart attacks.[2]

WAYS TO RELIEVE STRESS

- Eating three balanced meals a day is necessary for long-term protection against the effects of stress. Avoid excess sugar, fats, caffeine and alcohol.

- Engage in a regular exercise program—non-work activities that require sustained exertion. Aerobic exercise that increases the pulse rate to around 130 beats per minute improves the efficiency of heart beats and lowers the resting pulse rate.

- Learn and practice relaxation. Take a deep breath with your eyes closed, concentrating on counting to five while excluding all other thoughts. Exhale slowly through pursed lips counting to five again. Repeat this activity five times, and it will result in a temporary lowering of the blood pressure and a sense of readiness to concentrate on the next task.

- Create and use support networks to build high-quality relationships. Studies show that maintaining solid interpersonal relationships on the job enhances good health in the face of prolonged high levels of stress. The risk of developing stress-related physical and psychological conditions increases when there are no ongoing relationships on or off the job.

- Follow through on the recommendations for prayer and belief, remembering to "Cast all your anxiety on him for he cares for you". (I Peter 5:7)

THE URINARY SYSTEM ♥ HEALTH & WELLNESS
Time Management

The productive use of time is central in the life of successful people. It creates order and focus in our lives, manages stress levels and promotes a positive outlook on life. Order requires an essential priority around which all other factors are grouped. Once you identify the purpose you want to achieve, the need for prioritizing the rest of the tasks and solutions for your way of life becomes more obvious.

The question to ask yourself is, "Am I achieving the life that I want for myself and my family?" Constant swinging between periods of frantic and pointless activity and periods of inertia and procrastination means that it is time to rethink your use of time—both in terms of your daily life and your long-range ambitions. While we have all been given twenty four hours in a day and seven days in a week, some people are much more fulfilled and successful than others, and that does not have to be so.

---

[2] USA Today 5/14/99, pg. 12A by Marilyn Elias

There are many resources in the library and on the Internet that give other advice on problems ranging from organizing your life and managing your time to organizing your closets. Following the filtration, elimination and excretion steps detailed in the section Commit to the Cause will help you get started by setting the focus for your life. Now get a pad of paper and write down tasks in order as they come up during the day. You may want to make one section to list tasks for work and another one for home, separating them with a tab. This pad should be small enough to conveniently carry with you at all times. Major tasks that will be time consuming should be broken down into smaller tasks. Behavior changing actions identified in the exercise should be factored into your daily plans.

You may find it more beneficial to use the list with everything on it as a master list and make a daily list of three to ten tasks from your master list. It is a satisfying feeling to be able to look back at a list at the end of the day or week and see the number of tasks that have been crossed off as completed. You will find that on some days you only want to accomplish the easier options, while on other days completing a challenging objective suits you just fine. You can actually measure the fact that you are moving forward, regardless of the pace. Completing tasks leads to accomplishing goals, which results in your feeling alive and vibrant.

A year ago, I had my adult son who was having "issues" in his life write down a list of goals to accomplish prior to his 30th birthday. He called me recently to tell me that he had run across the list, and as he read it to me the pride and satisfaction in his voice were priceless when he told me that he had accomplished most of them already. I congratulated him and told him to write another list starting with the goals he had not met and add more.

Procrastination is putting off work. It is often caused by setting impossibly high standards for yourself. You know you procrastinate if you: can't get started, you putter and mutter in the morning rather than do or you finish the project at the last minute. To work through this tendency, break down the project into very small tasks that can be done in five minutes or less. You will tend to do it when you know it can be completed quickly.

"Behold, I have longed after thy precepts;
quicken me in thy righteousness.
This is my comfort in my affliction (suffering),
for thy word hath quickened me." (Psalm 119:40&50)

CHAPTER SUMMARY

THERE ARE THREE FUNCTIONS OF THE URINARY SYSTEM THAT ARE ESSENTIAL TO NOTE IN SETTING GOALS FOR OUR LIVES:

- Filtration – Occurs when our blood is forced through tiny strainers in the kidneys, separating out excess water and chemicals. This excess is called "filtrate." Filtration of our life styles occurs when we list our values and beliefs, then make another list of everything that we do. The things we do that are done in excess, or those that do not match our beliefs and values, are "filtrate," or excess baggage.

- Reabsorption – Occurs when specific amounts of the "filtrate" are reabsorbed into the system because there is a need for a little of it.
    - Reabsorption in life is when we make adjustments in the amount of time spent on some activities and add others that will enrich our lives while identifying other practices for elimination.

- Excretion – Occurs when the excess and waste in the "filtrate" are eliminated from the kidneys and the body.
    - Excretion in our daily lives is the process whereby we let go of practices and habits identified as waste to allow time to commit to meaningful activities that enhance our lives and the lives of others.

STRESS & TIME MANAGEMENT

- Stress comes from factors that occur in the workplace and at home by real and perceived expectations placed upon ourselves and from others.

- Positive stressors motivate us to achieve, while negative stressors can push one beyond physical and emotional limits.

- Negative stress is relieved by eating a balanced diet, aerobic exercise, relaxation and by developing relationships at and away from the work environment and by prayer and belief.

- The productive use of time is central in the life of successful people.

- Itemizing tasks to accomplish on a single pad or notebook and making daily lists from it helps us to maintain focus and attain our goals.

- Completing small tasks means achieving goals, which leads to success.

TIME MANAGEMENT WORKSHEET

LIST ACTIVITIES	TIME SPENT ON THE ACTIVITY	BELIEF OR VALUE THE ACTIVITY SUPPORTS

INDEX

Smith Hughes & Associates, Inc.
P.O. Box 388 Ashland, Ohio 44805

ORDER FORM

QUICKENED Made Alive! Spirit Soul Body
By Stephanie O. Hughes

Cost: $22.50 each X ____ = _______ + 6% Tax = _____ + $4.00 S&H = ______

Name: ____

Address: ____

City: ________________________ **State:** __________ **Zip:** ________

Telephone: ____________________ **E-mail:** ____________________

Telephone Orders: (800)247-6553 Have your credit card ready.

E-mail Orders: www.order@bookmaster.com

Internet Orders: www.atlasbooks.com

Fax Orders: Send this form to (419)281-6883

Postal Orders: Mail this form to: Smith Hughes & Associates Inc.
P.O. Box 388
Ashland, Ohio 44805

Payment: □ Check □ Visa □ Master Card □ Discover

Card Number: ____________________ **Name on Card:** ____________________

Expiration Date ____________________________ Exp. Date: __________

Signature: ____